HOW CAN THIS BE?

This story is a gift.
He who has eyes let him see,
He who has ears let him hear.

KEN ELLSWORTH

Inks and Bindings
888-290-5218
www.inksandbindings.com
orders@inksandbindings.com

I would like to give thanks to some very special people: my ex-wife Deb; my daughters, Jenny, Jackie, Kristy, and Kassie; Luke Beling, Kristy's husband; and Gina Collins.

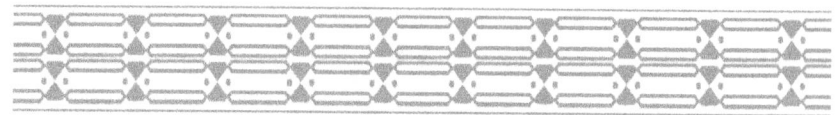

Why Did I Write This?

It was July 17, 2012; my heart was failing. The doctors said that I needed a new heart, a transplanted heart from a donor. How could this be? Why me? I was sixty-nine years old; I had run a good race, and I was at peace with myself and my Creator. Should I receive a heart, or should I let it go to another person? I have done my best. What should I do?

There are two parts to this story. I assume that you will read the first part of this book and my testament of what I did. My story is all about how I became a follower of Jesus Christ. The second part is what I have learned and how and why I learned it.

This is what I want to share with my family, friends, and anyone who is seeking the truth of Jesus. I want to talk about what is the truth and how it affects your faith in this world, and who is God? What do you believe?

My title of this book is *How Can This Be?* This is a classic way that Jews teach through stories and parables; they teach through contrasting ideas. This story is a gift. He who has eyes, let him see. He who has ears, let him hear. How can this be? It just is. What is faith, and where does it come from?

Now in 2024, I am eighty-one years old. As I look back, I see how hard it has been to see the truth. What is the truth? Most people, including myself, believe what we think is the truth. *Believe* is a verb, a tricky word. You can believe either good or not good and change from one to the other. *Belief* and *faith* are both nouns. While we can have beliefs that are true or not true, our faith we hold to be true. We have been given free will to choose what we believe. However, we have been born into a place in time, culture, history, language, and family that all influence our free will, and therefore, to choose can be complicated. I learned that there are two choices regarding who I am: the world's view and God's view. The mindset of this world is built on the wisdom and knowledge of men. This worldview can be good or bad, and we are here to choose what we believe. God's view is that the wisdom of man is foolish in God's eyes. That is why He sent His Son, Jesus Christ, to this world. The Son of Man is totally natural like us, and the Son of God is almighty. How can this be? How can He be both a man and God?

Jesus said in John 8:32, "And you will know the truth, and the truth will set you free." This was my dilemma: Do I trust my faith in myself, or do I trust my faith through Him? Will I just put my faith in the mindset of this world? Or will I receive my faith from Him as a gift through His grace? He said in Matthew 6:33–34, "But seek first His kingdom and His righteousness, and all these things will be added to you." Will it be my will or His will?

In 2001, the doctors reached a verdict and ultimatum: only a new heart would save my life. I made a declaration to God. I told Him that if He gave me a new heart, I would preach the gospel of grace and truth, share the story of His faithfulness in my life, and use my golf abilities to help others. It wasn't a bargain, as some seem to think God's hand works. I didn't see it as Him scratching my back so that I could scratch His. Rather, my declaration was an offering of thanks, the way a son chooses to honor his father from a place of love, not duty. This is a statement, not an invoice. So I told Jesus the same way He told His Father: "Not my will, but Your will be done."

In 1996, I went to sleep like on any normal night. But around 3:00 a.m., I had a dream. I woke up abruptly, and I had to write it down. It was a poem. I had never written or thought about anything like this before. How could this be? "Behold" is the poem's title, and it plays a major role in this story. All the words of this poem came from scriptures in the Bible.

Another time in 1999, during an afternoon nap, I woke up from the nap and was totally confused. What happened? I had a stroke. My ex-wife took me to a hospital, and I could not speak. About two weeks later, I was diagnosed with a hole in my heart, causing the stroke, and I was told that I would not be able to speak again. A friend of mine, Kristy Miller, came to see me, and we prayed together. At the end of this time, she said, "Ken, God is not finished with you yet." How could this be? The Holy Spirit showed me that His time and my time are different. I remember Jesus told Peter, "Peter, this is not your time to know this." Secrets in time are crucial, and there will be more on the subject of *time* in this story. These are some of the secrets and the mysteries of my life.

Now in 2022, after time, searching, and praying, I decided to tell my story. I am now eighty-one ears old. I have a question: Are we here through evolution, or are we created by God or gods? We have free will, and we can choose what we believe. I believe a person's identity is crucial, and we are here to be tested and to make a choice; we have free will. Your choice: the wisdom of God or the wisdom of man. The world view or God's view?

This is why I wrote this story, for my family, my friends, and for anyone who will be willing to see with their eyes and hear with their ears and find the real truth from God's Word. Not from the mind of the flesh (world), but to understand and believe the truth through your heart. God is real, and Satan is real. Jesus Christ came here to save us from Satan's lies. We will be judged as Satan himself will be judged. The world will end. But your soul and your spirit will live eternally. Death is not dead; we could be born again into God's kingdom.

So this is what I've learned: Fight the right fight. Seek and speak the truth. Matthew 6:33–34: "But seek first His kingdom and His righteousness, and all these things will be added to you. So do not worry about tomorrow, for tomorrow will care for itself. Each day has enough trouble of its own." Again, Jesus said in Matthew 7:19–21, "Do not store up for yourselves treasures on earth, where moth and rust destroy, and where thieves break in and steal. But store up for yourselves treasures in heaven, where neither moth nor rust destroys, and where thieves do not break in or steal. For where your treasure is, there your heart will be also."

OK, if I choose Jesus, then what should I do? He said, "Come and see, hear and learn, and love God."

> You shall love the Lord your God with all your heart,
> and with all your soul, and with all your mind.
> (Matthew 22:37–39)

This is the great and foremost commandment. The second is this:

> You shall love your neighbor as yourself.

Here is my question: God chose us before the foundation of this world through His love; can we love and choose Him back?

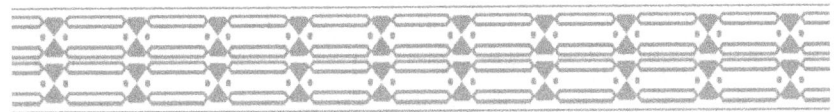

Contents

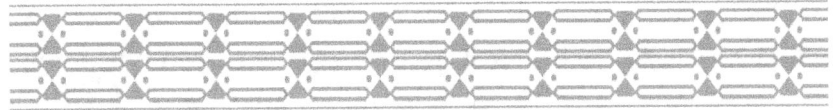

My Story

I was born in Chicago but grew up in Los Angeles, where the air is warm and the seasons are predictable. My heart beat to the rhythm of its own desire. I would only discover this disease, known as tachycardia, much later in life.

My mother and father loved each other. We were a Lutheran family even though Mom was a devout Catholic, excommunicated by her church for marrying Dad in a Lutheran church. But even Catholic law could not stop her stubbornness. She continued to attend mass, take communion, and pray for my sister and me.

My father's gospel was sports. He created my love for athletic competition. My first golf swing was guided by his hands. His teaching method was simple: He'd leave me at the course with a set of clubs, then give me the choice of admiring the scenery or finding my golf swing. Cancer killed him when I was in my thirties, but he knew God. On his deathbed, he rested in the grace of Jesus Christ.

I excelled as an athlete. My early teenage years brought the prospect of joining the Pittsburgh Pirates' minor-league program as a pitcher. If not for my first love, basketball, I believe I could have done well and maybe pitched in the majors, but my desire was for basketball. In 1960 and 1961, I made the Los Angeles all-city basketball team, which led to a scholarship offer from the University of Utah during my senior year of high school. The Utes had been ranked as high as third in the nation at that time. This distinction moved me to accept their offer, an open door into a boyhood dream.

Before moving to Utah, I experienced a great senior year. My high school brought prospects coming from every direction. One of the ways came by means of the church; another by way of a special girl, Gina, the first girl I ever loved. The church taught me about God. I traveled a narrow road of faithfulness, remaining thankful for the gifts He had given me. Gina was in my fondest memories of 1961. We spent warm summer nights sneaking across the prettiest golf courses in Palos Verdes—walking, talking, and enjoying life together. As my senior year came to an end, it broke my heart to leave her, but we promised to write and call. At Utah, every thought and emotion needed to be focused toward my basketball career.

Things began to unravel during my sophomore year at Utah. In those days of 1963, we had freshman teams before anyone could play on the varsity team. But the next year, my position on the team felt like wet cement taking years to dry. One of my friends said I was a great player. He also pointed out I had the mind of a wandering sailor with no compass. The cold, wooden bench became a familiar place during games. The coach of Utah deceived me. He told me I was the best outside shooter he had ever seen and that I would be great in his system. So why was I not playing? I asked him why! He said, "I do not play sophomores." Why did he not tell me? So I left Utah and went back to LA. I was mad, sad, and angry. That was the first time I learned about truth.

During this time, it felt like Gina was more than two states away. We'd slowly drifted apart. All I held of her was a photograph in my wallet. Our sun had set, and I blamed God for all of it. *Why did I lose her? Why was I sitting on the bench? I did nothing wrong. I kept Your laws.* And now I was mad, and I felt alone. I was twenty years old and weary of waiting. His voice felt further away than the moon. I decided to take control. From then on, I'd become the captain of my own ship. I was ready to make a move. The call of competition was louder than a thunderstorm. I couldn't bear to sit another minute on the lowly bench at Utah, so at the end of my second season with the

Utes, I accepted a scholarship from Pepperdine University in Malibu, California. I was sure I'd only have to wait one short summer before I would be back on track.

At home in Los Angeles, waiting through the summer before the fall semester brought a heavy sense of loss. Memories of Gina and hopes of basketball rushed into my mind at each familiar stop sign and on each high hill. Time was a thief. The more I had, the more it stole. Summer stood still; bright, misty mornings melted into hot noon pavements. The afternoons were cooled by shade and sea then faded into black. Each day repeated, separated by a few moments of rest and freedom.

The occasion of my dismal summer state led me into my garage. There I found my golf clubs dusted in spiderwebs. Golf was my third sport, a way to pass the time and, now, to fight the gloom. That summer, golf also strengthened my connection with my father. My favorite boyhood memories were of our time together, finding my swing, using clubs double my size. In some ways, golf was like a bridge into my father's heart. Together or alone, after a round of golf, I felt near to him.

So in the summer of 1963, I decided to play golf. I practiced and worked hard on my swing, and I liked to compete. My short game improved. Because of my height and length in my swing, I could drive the ball further than anyone on the course. The stamina and focus required over eighteen holes challenged me, and it was a time to learn sports and life. I entered the Los Angeles Amateur Championship. I was confident but out of place. The competition was stiff. But I did play some tournaments in junior golf, so I had some history about tournament golf, and I knew the rules. On the final day, I played well, but I could not catch the leader, and I finished in second place. But I was pleased. The coach from Cal State approached me with an offer after the tournament: "Come and play golf for me, Ken." After explaining to him that I was primarily a basketball player and preparing for the fall semester at Pepperdine University, he said, "Well, I'll tell our basketball coach we have a ringer, and you can play both golf and basketball." So I accepted their offer—a scholarship to play both golf and basketball for California State University, Los Angeles.

My junior and senior years were my most successful collegiate years as an athlete. Golf had overtaken basketball as my dominant sport. The progress I'd made in two years was really special. Our golf team finished second in the NCAA Championship Division I during my junior year. As a senior, I won three college tournaments, as well as the individual conference championship. I was All-Conference in basketball and All-American in golf.

Upon finishing from California State, I qualified for the PGA Tour. In my first tournament, I played in the Hawaiian Open. I shot 11 under par, and I led the tournament after 36 holes. In the last round of the tournament, I was paired with Lee Trevino. Lee had just won the United States Open, and now I was playing with him in the featured group. It turns out that Lee had the lead at the 14th hole, but I was just one shot back. The wind was howling from right to left. I lined up at the right trap, thinking that surely the wind would push the ball to the left. Right—no, it was not to be. I was playing in my first PGA Tour tournament, trying to beat Lee Trevino in the Hawaiian Open. Well, sure enough, when the ball was in flight, the wind just stopped. The ball went exactly where I tried to hit it, and it ended up buried in the lip of the right bunker. The results on the 14th hole: I made 6, Lee birdied 3. Trevino won the tournament. But it still ended up being the best day ever.

From 1968 to 1972, I played well, and my confidence grew. Summers extended to the majority of the year as I traveled from city to city, course to course, competing in one of the world's grandest spotlights. The Bridgestone Golf Classic, held in Japan in 1970, would be my final and most memorable ascent. The eastern course favored finesse over brute strength. Fairways were tree-line thin, and intricate sand traps protected fast greens. Nobody expected me to do well in Japan. But the Japanese onlookers cheered in amazement. The modest course complemented my game: long drives and my short game set putts for birdies. The par fours followed this script, and the par fives presented occasions for eagles. My swing felt as easy as breathing; I was in the flow. At the end of the first eighteen holes, I broke the course record with 64, 8 under par.

The crowd was at my back even though the Japanese native, the tournament favorite, remained close on my heels for the majority of the tournament. By the final nine holes, I had established a comfortable lead and finished with confident playing. I clinched the title, the grandest tournament of my career. Japanese fans were used to solemn jubilations, so when I shook the champagne and hosed their faces with bubbly, they jumped out from their cultural shells and burst into cheers. The tournament director presented me with a check for $10,000 and an additional $500 for breaking the course record.

Soon after my victory in Japan, I was approached by a man who claimed he could fix my swing. I didn't think it needed any fixing. But my sights were on stardom, better than good, so I bought into the age-old lie that many men and women have believed since the birth of the world: the lie that Adam and Eve believed in the garden of pleasure: "You are not—so you must do—in order to become." This is Satan's lie; shame is Satan's secret (i.e., "You are not good enough"). And like our first father and mother, after believing and acting on that lie, I also fell from the top of the world. My swing was stolen. Or rather, I gave it away to an idea sponsored by greed. In 1974, I lost my card to compete on the PGA Tour. My ranking dropped outside of the top 100 players in the world. I played small tournaments to stay afloat, winning chump change, but every time I tried to get my PGA card back, I lost by a shot or two, spinning my wheels with no place to go.

In 1976, I married Deb, a pretty girl from Arizona whom I met after a golf tournament. Her support and love became my bedrock. She stuck with me in trying times and encouraged my golf pursuits with confidence. But I had to be honest with myself and think of her as well. My career as a professional golf player could no longer support us, so I began to look for an alternative way to make a living. I landed a job at an impressive golf course in Wisconsin as their head professional. I worked diligently for two years, building up their program and managing their pro shop. My hunger for success as a PGA professional grew. I applied for the head professional position at one of Minnesota's top country clubs. I snagged the job as well as a hefty pay raise.

By 1980, I was married to a beautiful wife, blessed with two beautiful daughters and two more to come as the years rolled on. My sturdy salary provided the luxury of buying a dream house, perfectly situated on a scenic lake. I was popular with the members of the country club, and I didn't think much about money or feel the pressure that it often puts on people. The country club's board of directors, however, could not be pleased. This was the only shade of black on my near-perfect picture. These men, who were my overseers, were in a constant state of disapproval. I struggled to live up to their expectations of me, and their opinions kept me from sleeping at night.

In slow moments in my boat, fishing on the lake, or on drives home when I'd turn the radio off, I'd feel hollow, like a luxury sports car with no engine: pretty on the outside, but empty and lifeless within. The roots of these barren feelings came mostly from a single lie that I had entertained and swallowed for almost all my life: "You are not, so you must do in order to become."

Beginning with my falling out with the coach at Utah, to the man who claimed he could fix my swing because he thought he had Hogan's secrets, and now the board of directors at the country club who wanted more from me, I had thoughts of being not quite good enough. Adding to this pressure was the unhappiness of Deb, who was stressed and unsatisfied with our marriage.

I was outside, shoveling snow in February of 1982, when I collapsed in defeat. Finally, the heavy thoughts of not measuring up overwhelmed me. I violently gathered snow, then hurled it as hard as I could against the garage door in frustration. It was my only response to the harassing thoughts in my head. My strength was finished, and I was completely bare of any power to overcome the problems surrounding me. I fell into the snow and stared into the cold winter sky. I thought on the day in Utah when I turned my back on God for a lonely, sinking ship of self. This gray Minnesota day was familiar but different: familiar because I had fallen short once again, but different because I had finally realized that no answer or way out lay within any part of my struggling self. So I rose from the snow and uncorked my ears, giving their attention to the sound of God. After a while, I started to see my whole life: Golf and sports were my source, and God had been my resource. But now I had fallen so low that I was willing to abandon my own efforts and give control back to God. God has the right to all control, but He never demands it. So I said, "If You are really here, my golf will be a resource and *You* will be my source." My path back to God was a subtle journey of discovering a gift He had given to me and to the entire world before the dawn of creation; the secret is my will versus God's will.

Grace was beyond my understanding. Everything that I had ever hoped and dreamed of had already been given to me through the man, Jesus Christ. His gift was free. He required no work from my hands. I realized that Jesus had given me a receipt and not an invoice, contrary to the way I had lived up until that point in time. I didn't have to work to be better anymore. I no longer bought into the lie that I had to do something or act in a certain way to receive something that I was lacking. Adam was perfectly like God and needed nothing before he ate the fruit. I had finally realized that I didn't need to eat any more fruit to become somebody I already was in Jesus Christ. I had been set free in my mind to know the gift that God had released through Jesus's death and resurrection on the cross. I mulled over Romans 11:6, and my life grew in satisfaction for the love of God: "But if it is by grace, it is no longer on the basis of works; otherwise, grace is no longer grace." I finally found out that in the beginning, I knew about Jesus, but that now I knew Him. To know Him is to see the mindset of men: worldview versus kingdom view.

Debbie and I sought help from a counselor, and the love and grace of God filled the cracks in our marriage. Our marriage improved for a while but would eventually fall apart, mostly because of me. Maybe she did not see the difference, but I did. Pastor Dave Johnson said, "You are a new person; the old things have passed away; because new things are to come" (2 Corinthians 5:17).

In 1987, the problems with the board of directors amplified. I was staring into a mirror, a familiar situation. I thought I had done no wrong, but circumstances were far from the pictures in my mind. In Utah, I ran from God to the control of my own hands, eventually slipping slowly into darkness. But twenty years of darkness is a sure way to teach a man about grace: to teach him what grace is not. The country club wanted to replace me with another golf professional. I was tempted to argue and defend my case, but I ran to God. I trusted in His grace, His gift of provision and life, regardless of my effort and strength, and I ended up staying at the country club.

Three years later, the pressure of being a head professional at such a prestigious country club had finally run its course. I kept myself from the vicious trap of people-pleasing, but even still, my shoulders grew heavy with a weight I no longer wanted to carry. It was time to leave. We bought a fishing resort on the Chippewa Flowage near Hayward, Wisconsin. It contained a simple family house and nine cabins with only time to rest and fish. It was heaven, and I was making enough money to get by, hosting families for their annual summer vacations or their brave winter getaways. Life was enjoyable for five years, surrounded by crystal lakes and tall, beautiful pines. Our income wasn't stable enough to keep the life we had been living. We sold the resort in 1995 and moved into the city of Hayward, no longer on its outskirts.

The loss of the resort, together with our lack of communication, strained our marriage and then broke it. Deb and I decided on divorce. The divorce brought turmoil to my days that followed. I questioned God. I agreed with Solomon in the book of Ecclesiastes: Vanity, vanity, all of life is just vanity. Why is life so hard, God? God's grace was present, though. He comforted me with the assurance that His love would never leave me, no matter the trial or weight of my decisions.

I returned to what I know best: the golf swing. I became the PGA professional director of Natural Golf schools. I listened and learned from Moe Norman, a man who could hit the golf ball pure as anyone, an honored member of the Canadian Hall of Fame. Natural Golf, as its name suggests, is an approach to learning the golf swing based on an individual's instincts instead of trying to mold or cement one ideal swing for every player. I enjoyed teaching from this perspective and still believe it is the only way for an individual to find his or her golf swing.

When Moe was five years old, he fell down and a car ran over the side of his head. He was never taken to a doctor. Later, his mom said that he was never the same. Whatever happened that day, nobody knows for sure. But without doubt, he had one of the most brilliant minds for the golf swing that I ever met. The ways he saw things and the knowledge that he shared with me were priceless. For five years, I traveled the country conducting Natural Golf schools and training other professionals in the understanding of the way that Moe Norman swung the golf club: "hit that ball with a stick." I made several appearances on the Golf Channel advocating the methods of Natural Golf. Teaching golf had never been more enjoyable and fulfilling.

In the year 1996 began the problems with my heart—the problems that had always been there but hardly surfaced until now. The doctors figured out that I had electrical problems. They placed a defibrillator and pacemaker in my left chest.

These health issues frightened me and served as a strong reminder of whose faith was keeping me: mine or His? Even faith is a gift from God. We often think that faith is our part and the rest is God's. If that were the case, we'd have a right to take credit for God's activity in our lives as the spark initiating His movement. Alternatively, when times of trouble come and the reality of circumstances seems impossible to overcome, how could we ever drum up enough faith for the breakthrough? "But now apart from the Law even righteousness of God is manifested, borne witness to by the Law and the Prophets, even the righteousness of God by faith in Jesus Christ for all those who believe" (Romans 3:21–22). During the discovery of my heart problems, I relied greatly on the faith of Jesus. I rested in His ability to believe on my behalf, causing my thoughts to be at peace. My health did not improve immediately. In fact, the opposite took place. The following seventeen years would be a downward spiral for the strength of my body until only death or a miracle would relieve its suffering. I carried on for four years with no incidents, and then the start of my collapse swept me from my feet.

In September 1999, only months before my next stint on the Golf Channel, I had a stroke. I lay down for an afternoon nap and woke with no vocabulary, save one word. I rushed to Debbie's house, only a block away, and beat on the door. Debbie responded to the knock and immediately drove me to the hospital. The only word to come from my mouth, as I rested helplessly in the hospital bed, was "Jesus." I repeated His name to the doctors, my family, and the nurses aiding my body. The doctors called it a miracle. Every medical reason suggested the loss of my entire vocabulary. But the name of Jesus transcends the area of the brain and is buried deep in a man's heart, beyond science and reason.

After two weeks, the doctors released me from their care. They said my language faculty would improve a little: Speaking, reading, and writing would improve for about six to nine months, then I'd hit a wall, unable to progress. Thanks to the help of Debbie, my daughters, a good friend, and the Holy Spirit, I surpassed the doctors' expectations. Today, my language ability is not where it used to be, but it's darn close. The poem that had come to me in a dream in 1996 became key in regaining my language skills.

After my stroke, I was unable to work and continued to reside in Hayward for several years under close supervision by medical personnel. The rhythm of my heart struggled, and my days felt fewer and nearer to death. In 2001, the doctors reached a verdict and ultimatum: Only a new heart would save my life. I was placed on the heart transplant list. It was a promise from my heavenly Father. I made a declaration to God. I told Him that if He gave me a new heart, I would preach the gospel of grace, share the story of His faithfulness in my life, and use my golf abilities to help others. It wasn't a bargain, as some seem to think God's hand works. I didn't see it as Him scratching my back so that I could scratch His. Rather, my declaration was an offering of thanks—the way a son chooses to honor his father from a place of love, not duty.

In 2005, my family moved to Rochester, Minnesota. Even though Debbie and I were divorced, our family remained very close. It would have been strange to be so far from them, so we left the clean air and tall pines for the city lights of Rochester. Immediately, I established a relationship with the doctors and nurses at the world-famous Mayo Clinic. Mayo Clinic is a premium health-care facility and hospital. From the moment I walked into the old downtown building, I was sure I was in the best medical hands the country could offer. And so began a pivotal part in my story—the start of my journey toward recovery.

After two years in the care of Mayo Clinic, waiting for an organ, my heart regained strength and consistency. The doctors removed me from the transplant list in 2005. I felt a mixture of peace and confusion at the announcement of their decision. I had been awaiting and expecting a new heart, only now to be taken off the list. But the news of improved cardiac rhythm was certainly reassuring and comforting. However, the days, weeks, and months that followed evidenced a steady decline of health, contrary to the doctors' thoughts and hopes. I experienced frequent dizzy spells and was confined to sitting inside for most of my days, hardly able to do anything at all. The stamina of my heart and its ability to pump blood through my body did not waver much; however, my cardiac rhythm increased in its inconsistency, skipping beats like a broken metronome.

Five years of battling up and down, here and there, from 2005 to 2010, almost broke the hope inside of me. Every contradiction in my body spoke as loud as a thunderstorm, "God has not healed you, and He will not heal you." A single thought and truth from the Holy

11

Spirit, however, extinguished accusations and kindled the fire of hope again, keeping me safe and secure in that dark night. The Holy Spirit began to speak to me about the timeless zone that He lives and exists in. When He spoke to Abram and changed his name to Abraham (the father of many nations), Abraham was old and did not have a single child. From then on, Abraham would introduce himself to people as the father of many nations. Abraham would think of himself as the father of many nations, a name contrary to the evidence of his days. In God's mind, Abraham was already the father of many nations, even before the birth of his first child. Time was not the author and supplier of this gift for Abraham; God was. Likewise, I learned to trust in God and not time. I was already healed as far as God was concerned, in the timeless zone, so I set my eyes and thoughts on this place and not the dwindling state of my body. This can be a hard concept to understand because of all the apparent contradictions we face. However, the question we need to ask ourselves is, when did God provide the forgiveness of sin? When did God provide the healing of our bodies? Can anything be added to the accomplishment of the cross? It was at the cross that complete provision for every need was given, and our place is to trust in that, not time or contradiction in front of us. Faith is the evidence of those things not yet seen.

In March 2010, on a scheduled doctor's visit, the medical staff at Mayo Clinic ran some tests and checkups, then discovered my heart was working at a rate of 15 percent of its expected workload. The doctors told me I had two months to live and that there was a new device that would sustain my life during those final two months and provide an outside chance of prolonging my days. The risks involved in installing the LVAD were minimal compared to the potential benefits for my body and proved to be lifesaving. As a result of receiving the LVAD, I would also regain an opportunity to be placed on the heart transplant list if everything went according to plan. The decision to undergo this procedure was a no-brainer. At the time, I thought that the LVAD might be God's method of healing, but looking back, I see that it was a necessary bridge to the eventual restoration that He had planned from the beginning.

The LVAD operates as an artificial heart motor, powered by batteries, to perform duties that an otherwise healthy heart would normally fulfill. My body, at first, responded incredibly well. I regained strength that had been far from me for almost ten years. So much pressure and strain were removed from my heart due to the help of the LVAD, resulting in a new surge of energy for my days. The device was awkward, and my children thought of me as the bionic man—half human, half machine—but its effectiveness added two years to my life. After about six months of carrying the LVAD, I dusted off my golf clubs and began to play and teach golf again. My swing felt very different, hindered by a battery pack over my shoulder and a wire coming out from my abdomen. But the joy of being on the course rejuvenated me. I didn't have the strength to walk nine holes, and on hot summer days, I had to stay inside, but worthy occasions to golf were almost impossible to deny. In the summer of 2010, I played golf at least once a week, sometimes twice, to the surprise and delight of my family and doctors. The year 2010 proved to be one of my healthiest years, and in my mind, I turned a corner. I wasn't close to full strength or health, but I no longer felt like a man waiting for death's day.

In the month of May, I was placed at the top of the heart transplant list. I was already on the list but made a jump to next in line. It's a strange thing waiting for a heart, knowing that somebody has to die so that I might live. Someone has to die so that I may live sounds like the same story: Jesus has to die so that I may live, born again to receive a new heart; old things go away, and all things are new. May passed, then June, without a single call from the doctor's office. In July, my name was taken from the top of the list, not for any reason other than standard procedure. Because my health was relatively stable, my name rotated on the list—from the top, to the middle, to the end, and back again. July felt like a cage fight with a lion. This might have been because of the heat or the sheer disappointment of not receiving my new heart. I hardly played any golf and stayed inside with the AC. Summer dragged and turned into fall, then winter, my heart doing mostly okay, but the waiting was tough.

In April 2012, the defibrillator in my left chest began to shock me on a more than regular basis. The purpose of these shocks was to slow my cardiac rhythm, to force my racing heart to a normal pace. The shocks frightened me at every moment. Unexpected bursts of electricity surging through one's body never become normal or an occurrence that one gets used to. The LVAD and defibrillator could no longer control the speedy engine of my heart. The doctors performed one more small surgery in hopes of slowing my cardiac rhythm. My name bounced, like a ping-pong ball, back to the top of the list with more warnings, explaining that only a new organ would keep me alive for longer than a few months. The doctor's words began to sound like a lunch siren— over and over, on time, without fail. A constant reminder of death is a sure way to lose confidence and hope, but I trudged on, waiting and praying for the heart that would keep me alive. The procedure to slow my rhythm worked for a while, but then my body caught on, my heart refusing to be tamed. The daily dosage of medicine increased, and with it, the side effects that left me dizzy, disoriented, and confused. In the past, these extremities warranted a visit to the emergency room to receive a shot of medicine or support from machines. So I called the medical team to let them know that I was coming in. This time, it was different. The nurses, then doctors, said they had no help for me—not because they weren't willing, but rather, every solution, other than providing me with a new heart, had been exhausted.

The months following April were filled with uncertainty. Thankfully, the shocks became less frequent, but any sudden change in the way my body felt left me paranoid and frightened. All I could do was hang on and hope against all doubt. And this I did for another three months. On July 28, 2012, I received a call from Mayo Clinic bearing news that would completely alter my life. They had a heart for me. They could not tell me where it came from or whom it had belonged to, only that it was en route for delivery.

"How fast can you get here, Mr. Ellsworth?" My apartment was only a block away from the hospital. I called my family, gathered my belongings, and rushed to the clinic as though my very life depended upon it. The thoughts, collecting in my mind, were many and various, charged with excitement and disbelief. *Is this really happening? And will it work? Will the heart match my body? Please, Lord, if it is Your will, let it be.*

I sat in the hospital bed, waiting for about four hours before the procedure took place. My family was with me and listened attentively to the doctors coming in and going out, performing their mandatory duties of communicating the risks and order of the transplant surgery. The small hospital room filled with nervousness and anticipation. But as time moved on, the reality of what was about to happen sank deeper into our minds, and peace with it. We prayed and asked God to guide the surgeon's hands and to fit the new heart perfectly into my body. I kissed my girls, then told them I'd be seeing them in the morning. Like any surgery, time passed in the blink of an eye, and I woke to pain, stiffness, and bewilderment. After three days of falling in and out of sleep, induced by the heaviest dose of pain medication, I understood the doctor's words—the success of the surgery. My new heart had taken to my body without any complications. God rescued me. He had given me a fresh start to life.

The first three weeks of my post-op recovery were incredibly painful. I lay in the hospital bed for what felt like an eternity, unable to walk and move because of the pain. After four weeks, I was released from the hospital with a new medicine prescription and a mandatory three-month watch to be implemented by my loved ones. During those three months, I slowly recovered and gained strength I thought I'd never know again. The healing was slow but with no hiccups or signs of my body rejecting the new heart.

Starting around the fourth month after surgery, I began to feel the way I used to when I was much younger, when I was healthy. As a result, I've been able to concentrate my days on the areas I love: God, my family, and golf. To spend years only trying to make it to the next day makes one grateful to experience every gift God has given. My golf swing is finding its way back, as are my plans to teach golf and to share the Good News of the Gospel of Christ.

Most importantly, I remember God. I remember, with every passing day, the gifts that He has given me. You have given me a new heart; You have given me life and more time. Thank You, Lord, for time. Whatever Your will is, whatever my time is, let me use it with You. My will and Your will are one.

This Is My Will and Testament

This is the end of my story. When did I know I was saved? Maybe when I was young and learned about God from a Lutheran church. Probably it was in 1982 when I gave up golf that controlled me. My whole life, I had been told how good I was. I was afforded money to play baseball and scholarships for basketball and golf. My identity and all my efforts were to be better. Is that bad? No, of course not. We want to do well, to be successful, to have good families. And I want to be good and truthful. But when I found out that I was in denial of the truth and the whole world was in denial of the truth, how could I learn and see and hear the real truth? Thank God, my wife said we needed to go to a church. Therefore, at the country club where I worked, I asked a coworker about churches. He said to go to the Open Door Church and ask for Jeff VanVonderen. So I did. I knew I could not fix myself; I knew I needed help. Was I willing to let go of my control in this life, and would I follow Jesus? This was my breaking point, my ultimate test: Why am I here, and what will I choose? Jesus, are you real? This is my test: Will I step forward and believe from my heart, not from my flesh, that Jesus is who he said he is? I started to see, and I started to hear the truth. Jesus is the Living Word. The apostle John says His name is Grace and Truth.

In 1983, there was an Easter breakfast with about two thousand men from many churches. The Open Door Church was aligned with the Christian and Missionary Alliance. There was a special speaker named Roosevelt Grier, who was an All-Pro from the Los Angeles Rams football team. He was huge, about 6'7" tall. After he spoke, he asked if there was anyone who wanted to receive Christ. When I went to the breakfast, I was alone, and I did not see anyone I knew. I was all the way in the back of the crowd. Immediately, I jumped up and walked all the way to the front. When Grier was finished praying with me, I started back through the tables. Grier yelled to me, "Hey, big guy" (I was 6'4"); he said, "Do it!"

I yelled back, "I am!" I did not say, "I will"; I said "I am." As I walked back to my table, I started to feel kind of weird! Why did I say that? I kept thinking I should have said, "OK," or "I will." When I said, "I am," it seemed like the wrong thing to say. I was just a baby in Jesus. I was not familiar with the Christian language. Many years later, I found out that God's name is I Am, and to this day, I do believe that it was not my voice that spoke. This did not come from my natural spirit; it came from the Spirit of truth from my heart. I spoke out in front of two thousand men, but this was a word or a prophecy for me, then I knew for sure I was a son of God.

At this time, I was just a baby in Christ, but the Holy Spirit taught me of God's Word. As a son of God, I agree with the apostle Paul's teachings in Galatians 2:20–21: "I have been crucified with Christ; and it is no longer I who live, but Christ lives in me; and the life which I now live in the flesh I live by faith in the Son of God, who loved me and gave himself up for me. I do not nullify the grace of God; for if righteousness comes through the Law (works), then Christ died needlessly." What Paul is saying here is that the law of Moses was like a mirror that shows us the difference between good and evil, right and wrong. Grace is a free gift, unmerited, unearned favor of God through His love, and His love is unconditional. The law shows me I am a sinner; I was not deceived by the truth of this world. I learned to fight the right fight, teach the truth, and share God's truth in His Word. Jesus is the Word, and His name is Grace and Truth. Ephesians 1:4–5 says, "Just as He chose us in Him before the foundation of the world, that we would be holy and blameless before Him. In love, He predestined us to adoption as sons through Jesus Christ to Himself according to the kind intention of His will." He stretches out His hands, and He says, "I chose you, I created you, I love you." Here, Jesus says, "This is My ring. Will you marry Me?"

And I say, "Yes." Therefore, Jesus says, "I pledge to you." Ephesians 1:13: "In Him, you also, after listening to the message of truth, the gospel for your salvation—having also believed, you were sealed in Him with the Holy Spirit of promise." For me, His promise was enough; in God's amazing time and in His grace, I choose Him. Therefore, I am going to be married to Him. I will learn the truth of who I am. And when I am ready, I will be married in and with His church, in His time. Our covenant will be, "All I have is His, and all He has is mine." This will also be our inheritance.

Remember this: God is faithful, and He chose me before the foundation of this world. I made my choice; I chose Him. The question is, how will you choose? The mindset of this world's view or from God's view?

> For I am convinced that neither death, nor life, nor angels, nor principalities, nor things present, nor things to come, nor powers, nor height, nor depth, nor any other created thing will be able to separate us from the love of God, which is in Christ Jesus our Lord. (Romans 8:38–39)

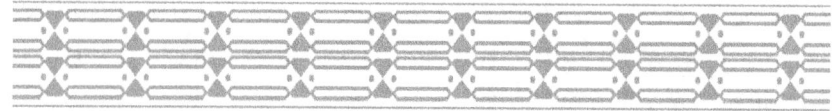

Now I Would Like to Share
What I Have Learned and Why

I would like to share some things that I have learned from 1990 until now. I am not a theologian; I am a charismatic nondenominational layman. I believe God's Word literally, and I do believe that the gifts of the Holy Spirit are true. However, I do not take the gift of prophecy lightly, and time and wisdom are crucial. I am referring to my poem. In 1996, I went to sleep, and I had a baffling dream. I dreamed the poem, and I wrote it down. What is this? How could this be? I'm not a poet. The poem just sat there until the year 2000. After my stroke in 1999, I was someone who could barely speak or write a sentence. On top of that, my heart was failing. I really had no vision for the future. So I found my poem, and I decided that I was going to find out what it meant.

> No temptation has overtaken you but such as is
> common to man, and God is faithful, who will not
> allow you to be tempted beyond what you are able,
> but with the temptation (test) will provide the way
> of escape also, so that you will be able to endure it.
> (1 Corinthians 10:13)

The poem was my way of escape from the test of my difficult period of time. Would I give up in despair, or would I stick it out? I began my Bible research of the poem, word by word. After you have read my story, my hope is that you can see, hear, and understand some of the things I have learned in my life and from my poem. How can this be? It just is.

> Who is God?
> I Am who I Am
> He just is
> Who is
> Jesus is now
> Who is now
> The Holy Spirit
> Who are you?
> I am me, and I am in You
> How can this be?
> It just is = faith

> Thank you, Jesus.

> Who was and is and who is to come, I Am who I
> Am. (Revelations 4:8)

Let's take a look at the Bible; this is a letter to the church: "Also we have obtained an inheritance, having been predestined according to His purpose, who works all things after the counsel of His will. In Him, you also, after listening to the message of truth, the gospel of your salvation, having also believed, you were sealed in Him with the Holy Spirit of promise" (Ephesians 1:11, 13).

If you do not read and learn the Word of God, the Bible, this may be very difficult to understand. This is why I wrote this story. I want you to know what I believe and why. All people in this world, except Jesus at the cross, are born into this world spiritually dead. "How can this be?" I believe we will be born, live, and die here. But my soul and my spirit will live forever, but where will it go? Will I have an inheritance with God or an inheritance in this world?

Let me confess why I was ignorant of the wisdom and knowledge about the creation of man into this world. Adam and Eve were the first creatures of man, images of or shadows of God. They were given free will and eternal life. What did they do with the free will that was given to them? I will explain this thoroughly later in this book. Here is another parable: "How can this be? I was lost, but now I have been found."

This is why we are here, to be tested on what you believe. God has already chosen for you the question. Your test is, will you choose Him back?

I would like to share six things with you:

1. How can a person who is dead spiritually be born again to the wisdom and knowledge of God?
2. This is what I learned and why I believe Jesus's Word.
3. This is my footprint of how I became a son of God.
4. And this is my motto: how I learned what I learned.
5. These are my steps from death to life. "How can this be? It just is."
6. I believe all of us will be judged by our faith = it just is. The question is, what is your faith and where did it come from?

My hope is to understand what Jesus said in John 8:32: "And you will know the truth, and the truth will make you free."

My motto is:

See it = wisdom/truth

Proverbs 1:7: "The fear of the Lord is the beginning of wisdom; Fools despise wisdom and instruction.

Know it = knowledge

Lamentations 3:25: "The Lord is good to those who wait for Him. To the person who seeks Him."

First Peter 1:3: "Blessed be the God and Father of our Lord Jesus Christ who according to His great mercy has caused us to be born again to a living hope through the resurrection of Jesus Christ from the dead."

Believe it = faith

John 5:24: "Truly, truly I say to you, he who hears My word and believes in Him who sent Me, has eternal life and does not come into judgment but has passed out of death into life."

This is a time to change. What do you believe?

Do it = learn to walk according to His will

John 16:6: "I am the way and the truth and the life; no one comes to the Father, but through me."

Ephesians 2:10: "For we are His workmanship, created in Christ Jesus for good works, which God prepared beforehand so that we would walk in them."

Own it = saved

Ephesians 1:4: "He chose us in Him before the foundation of the world, that we would be holy and blameless before Him."

I am here to be tested; will I choose Him as my Lord and Savior or not?

The wisdom of this world comes from the flesh minds of men. But the wisdom of God comes from the soul of your heart.

In the pages to come, I have organized what I have learned and my progression in belief in faith, according to these five areas of my motto, and I have linked each area to specific sections of my poem "Behold," which appears on the next page.

"Behold"

Behold the Lord Thy God
Jehovah the Great I Am
Creator of the Universe
Who became our Holy Lamb

Behold the Lord Thy God
Whose grace abounds to thee
He is the Son of Man
And His Truth has set you free
Free—from the wages of sin
Free—from the grasp of shame
Free—from death within
By the power of His name

Behold the Lord Thy God
Jehovah the Great I Am
Author of the promise
Given to Abraham
Given—in His covenant
Set free from sin and strife
Given—in His sacrament
His blood that gives us life

Behold the Lord Thy God
Who chose us from the start
His mercies never-ending
His love sets us apart

Apart—from this fallen place
Apart—from all defeat
Apart—by his gift of grace
In Him we are complete

Behold the Lord Thy God
Jehovah is His name
The Great Eternal One
The first, the last, the same

Behold the Lord Thy God
Creator of the light
That we should walk by faith
And not by worldly might
Walk – as a brand new creature
Walk – with a brand new heart
Walk – with trust in your teacher
And His Spirit will do His part

Behold the Lord Thy God
You oh Ancient of Days
Sovereign from the start
You mold us in your ways
You told me not to fear
To get strength from you on High
Before – I listened with my ear
But now – I see you with my eye

Trust not in things both seen and heard
I am a God who cannot lie
Through the Gospel power in my Word
I will meet you in the sky

25

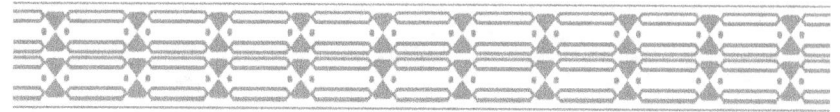

See It

The Problem, What Is Truth

From my story:

Things began to unravel during my sophomore year at Utah. In those days of 1963, we had freshman teams before anyone could play on the varsity team. But the next year, my position on the team felt like wet cement taking years to dry. One of my friends said I was a great player. He also pointed out I had the mind of a wandering sailor with no compass. The cold, wooden bench became a familiar place during games. The coach of Utah deceived me. He told me I was the best outside shooter he had ever seen, and I would be great in his system. So why was I not playing? So I asked him why! He said, "I do not play sophomores." Why did he not tell me? So I left Utah, and I went back to LA. I was mad, sad, and angry. That was the first time when I learned about truth.

From my poem:

Behold the Lord Thy God
Jehovah the Great I Am
Creator of the Universe
Who became our Holy Lamb
Behold the Lord Thy God
Whose grace abounds to thee

He is the Son of Man
And His Truth has set you free

How Can This Be?

What is the difference between the wisdom of man versus the wisdom of God? How can this be? The apostle Paul wrote a letter to the church of the Corinthians. Paul was concerned with spiritual and moral abuse, which led to divisions within the church. The causes of divisions within the church in Paul's day were the following:

- The misunderstanding of God's message of the cross.
- The misunderstanding of the Holy Spirit.
- The stunting of spiritual growth.

Not only was this a problem for Paul then, but it is a problem for me right now. Our churches have become secular in their culture, and the message of the cross is being lost. This is the difference between the wisdom of God and the wisdom of this world. Paul will tell you, fools become wise, and the wise are fools; the wisdom of man is foolishness in God's eyes.

Therefore, Paul says in 1 Corinthians 2:1–5 (KJV), "And I, brethren, when I came to you, came not with excellence of speech or wisdom, declaring unto you the testimony of God. For I determined not to know anything among you, save Jesus Christ, and Him crucified. And I was with you in weakness, and in fear, and in much trembling. And my speech and preaching was not with enticing words of man's wisdom but in demonstration of the Spirit and of power, that your faith should not stand in the wisdom of men but in the power of God."

First Corinthians 2:9–10: "But as it is written, things which eye hath not seen, nor ear heard, and which have not entered into the heart of man, all that which God hath prepared for them that love Him. For to us God hath revealed them through the Spirit; for the Spirit searches all things, yea, even the deep things of God."

We have all been born dead spiritually. We don't see, and we don't hear what God has prepared for us. The mindset of the world is based on the wisdom and knowledge of men. However, Paul says in Romans 12:2–3, "And be not conformed to this world: but be ye transformed by the renewing of your mind… For through the grace given unto me, I say to every man among you not to think of himself more highly than he ought to think, but to think soberly, as God hath dealt to every man the measure of faith."

That is why Jesus said you must be born again. John 3:3–8: "Jesus answered Nicodemus, 'Verily, verily, I say unto thee, unless a man be born again, he cannot see the kingdom of God.' Nicodemus saith unto Him, 'How can a man be born when he is old? He cannot enter a second time into his mother's womb and be born again, can he?' Jesus answered, 'Verily, verily, I say unto thee, unless a man is born of water and of the Spirit, he cannot enter the kingdom of God. That which is born of the flesh is flesh; and that which is born of the Spirit is spirit.'"

Notice here, the capital *S* is the Holy Spirit, and the small *s* is the natural spirit of man. "Marvel not that I said unto thee, ye must be born again. The wind blows where it wishes, and thou hearest the sound of it, but cannot tell where it comes from and where it goes; so is every one that is born of the Spirit." How can this be? *It just is.*

My question is, who am I, who is God, and who is the Son of Man and the Son of God? And who is the Holy Spirit, and what does He do? So I asked God, and this is what He said to my heart: Seek first the righteousness of God, then ask, and it will be given; seek, and you will find; knock, and it will be opened. For everyone who asks receives, and he who seeks finds, and to him who knocks, it will be opened. Trust Jesus, for He is the way, the truth, and the life. This is what I found.

When I was born in 1943, I was blessed that I could see with my eyes and hear with my ears. But later in my life, I found out that I was ignorant of the fact that I was born dead spiritually, that my mind was a bridge between my physical brain and the soul and the spirit. My body and my brain were flesh, and I was made from elements of this world. But my soul, my spirit, and my mind were spirit, and they were from a different realm. How can this be? Who am I, why am I here, and what should I do in this world? This is the mystery of this world.

Is there a higher power? Is there a god or gods? Maybe there is a natural evolution. Maybe there is an idol or an idea of community intelligence. This mindset of man is to make things better in this world, and thus we will grow into a higher power. And finally, there are cults of religious beliefs in a god. Here their works will be tested and judged according to their efforts and their works. This is the mindset of this world. This is the wisdom and knowledge of man's flesh.

Back to the letter of Paul to the church in 1 Corinthians 1:18–31, the Word and truth of God: "For the word of the cross is foolishness to those who are perishing, but to those who are being saved it is the power of God. For it is written, 'I will destroy the wisdom of the wise, and the cleverness of the clever I will set aside.' Where is the wise man? Where is the scribe? Where is the debater of this age? Has not God made the foolish the wisdom of the world? For since in the wisdom of God the world through its wisdom did not come to know God, God was pleased through the foolishness of the message preached to save those who believe. For indeed Jews ask for signs, and Greeks search for wisdom; but we preach Christ crucified, to Jews a stumbling block and to Gentiles foolishness, but to those who are the called, both Jews and Greeks, Christ the power of God and the wisdom of God. Because the foolishness of God is wiser than men and the weakness of God is stronger than men. For consider your calling, brethren (Christian believers in Christ), that there were not many wise according to the flesh, not many mighty, not many noble; but God has chosen the foolish things of the world to shame the wise, and God has chosen the weak things of the world to shame the things which are strong, and the base things of the world and the despised, God has chosen the things that are not, so that He may nullify the things that are, so that no man should boast before God. But by His doing you are in Christ Jesus, who became to us wisdom from God, and righteousness and sanctification, and redemption, so that just as it is written, 'Let him who boasts, boast in the Lord.'"

This might be hard to understand. If you are not a true believer in Christ, or if you don't believe that the Word of Jesus is true, then you have been deceived, and you did not seek to find or ask for the gift of God and the indwelling of the Holy Spirit. If your eyes did not see and if your ears did not hear the truth of the cross, then the truth of the cross is foolishness to those who are perishing, but to those who are being saved, it is the power of God through the light of life, through Jesus Christ. And when the power of the resurrection was fulfilled and Jesus left this world, He sent back the Comforter, the Holy Spirit, to lead us out of darkness and to see the way back to reconciliation in a relationship with our Father. This is why I am here: to be tested as to what I believe.

This is what I believe and why! I have been born into this world, but later, when I was older, I was born again a second time. This birth was not from the flesh of this world; it came from the Spirit to my spirit. I was given a gift from God's grace and mercy for anyone who believes in His name. Jesus Christ is the Son of God. This is why I am here: to share the truth of Jesus and the power of the resurrection of the cross. I have accepted the gift of God so that the Holy Spirit dwells in me through Jesus Christ. Now I can read and understand God's Word with the help of the Spirit of Truth (Holy Spirit). Now I have a way, a path from the Spirit of Truth to Jesus Christ, the mediator at the right hand of our Father.

When I pray and have no words to say, the Holy Spirit knows my heart, and the Son of Man shares my thoughts with our Father. The Lord will reveal His truth as He will. Why am I here, and what should I do? Now I am here to learn, grow, and believe who I am. The mystery in this world is to seek what is the truth, how to find it, and what is the real truth. Now I have even more questions about what is truth. Where will I go, and who is God, and who is Jesus? Are they who they claimed to be?

Who is Jesus? He is called by many names, but I would like to focus on just a few. Moses asked God, "What is your name?" and God said, "I Am who I Am." The whole Bible was written about the "I Am who I Am."

> In the beginning was the Word, and the Word was with God, and the Word was God. He was in the beginning with God. All things came into being by Him, and apart from Him, nothing came into being that has come into being. In Him was life, and the life was the light of men. And the light shines in darkness, and the darkness did not comprehend it. (John 1:1–5)

With all of the mysteries of God in this world, this is the question of all people: Who is Jesus? He claims to be a son of Mary as a human person, the Son of Man. However, John 1:1–5 says He (Jesus) is the Word, and the Word was with God from the beginning, and all things came through Him. He is life, and the light of men. And the light shines in darkness, and the darkness does not comprehend it.

How can this be? How can a normal human being in the flesh, a son of Joseph and Mary, be born into this world to Mary, a virgin? Jesus was fully human and fully divine, the Son of Man (Matthew 27:43) and the Son of God (Mark 14:62), the bridge between the flesh and the Spirit. There are a lot of scriptures about "I Am." The one I will focus on is John 14:6: "I am the way, and the truth, and the life; no one comes to the Father but through Me."

Let's take a look at the parts of this scripture. I am the way. Jesus says in Matthew 7:13–15, "Enter by the narrow gate; for the gate is wide, and the way is broad that leads to destruction, and many are those who enter by it. For the gate is small, and the way is narrow that leads to life, and few are those who find it. Beware of the false prophets who come to you in sheep's clothing, but inwardly are ravenous wolves." Jesus is the way to learn and understand the truth.

I am the truth. Remember John 1:1: "In the beginning was the Word, and the Word was with God, and the Word was God." Jesus is the Word and the Truth because He was with God before the beginning of this world. In God's time, Jesus was not a man of this world.

The last part of this scripture is, "I am the life." Now back to John 1:1–5: "In Him was life, and the life was the light of men. The light shines in the darkness, and the darkness did not comprehend it." Here is the problem of the wisdom of man versus the wisdom of God. If God is real, then we have to know that Satan is real also.

Let us take a look at the creation of this world from God's Word:

Genesis 1:1–4: "In the beginning, God created the heavens and the earth. The earth was formless and void, and darkness was over the surface of the deep, and the Spirit of God was moving over the surface of the waters. Then God said, 'Let there be light,' and there was light. God said that the light was good and separated the light from the darkness."

Genesis 1:26: "Then God said, 'Let Us (notice: Us) make man in Our image, according to Our likeness.'"

Genesis 2:1: "Thus the heavens and the earth were completed, and all their hosts."

Genesis 2:7–9: "Then the Lord God formed man of dust from the ground and breathed into his nostrils the breath of life, and man became a living being."

When Adam was placed into the garden of this world, he was made complete in all things. In Genesis 2:17, God commanded, "But from the tree of the knowledge of good and evil you shall not eat, for in the day that you eat from it you shall surely die." Adam had all things, especially free will and eternal life. So, God told him everything is good except do not eat of that tree because you will know the difference between good and evil, and then you will die.

Genesis 2:18: "Then the Lord God said, 'It is not good for man to be alone; I will make him a helper suitable for him.'"

Genesis 2:24–25: "For this reason, a man shall leave his father and his mother, and be joined to his wife; and they shall become one flesh. And the man and his wife were both naked and were not ashamed." This part here, "naked and not ashamed," is a very important thought. They had not sinned, but then Satan, the serpent, showed up and tempted them to sin, to eat from the tree of life in order to gain the knowledge of good and evil. The implication of this came from Satan's offer to be like God. Therefore, they bought the lie, and they ate the fruit, and immediately they had the consciousness of sin. So they took leaves of plants to cover their nakedness, and they hid themselves because they knew the difference between good and evil, and they were ashamed. They understood the power of sin.

God will not allow sin in His presence. Notice here: they were naked and not ashamed, but they ate, and then they hid and put on leaves because they were ashamed. So now they were lost to God, and they and all men afterward would live and die in this world.

I believe that is why we are here, to choose what to believe: Is God real? Is Satan real? Are there angels of good and evil? These spirits are living beings, and they roam in different realms. They both have access to this world, and they are here to fight in this spiritual war to win the souls of men. Which one will you choose: man's wisdom of this world, which has deceived the minds of men, or the wisdom of God through His Word?

Most people, but not all, seek to find a way to a higher power. All of us know deep down in our hearts that we are not perfect and we make mistakes. Our behaviors can be good, bad, or ugly. If we had a chance to undo our mistakes, most people would try. No one wants to carry that burden of shame. That is why this world is built on the idea or philosophy of the higher power. But this type of philosophy can be built on shame. Some philosophies of man can be good. But the wisdom of this world is foolishness in His (God's) eyes.

The only way for man to enter the presence of God's wisdom is through Jesus Christ. John 14:6: "I am the way, and the truth, and the life; no one comes to the Father but through Me."

Jesus is our mediator; he is our bridge; he is the Son of Man and the Son of God; he is both. He is one part of the Trinity, three persons of the Godhead. Here I want to talk about the thirty-three years of Jesus's time in this world. He was born in Bethlehem from the womb of the Virgin Mary. He was the Son of Man and the Son of God. He was the mediator from the Son of God and the bridge to the Son of Man. He was the way, the truth, and the life. He was here to share the wisdom and the knowledge of God through His Word. He was the straight path to enlighten our minds.

And Jesus said in Matthew 5:14–17, "You are the light of the world. A city set on a hill cannot be hidden. Nor does anyone light a lamp and put it under a basket, but on the lampstand; and it gives light to all who are in the house. Let your light shine before man in such a way that they may see your good works and glorify your Father in heaven. Do not think that I came to abolish the Law or the Prophets; I did not come to abolish but to fulfill." And His Word and His Truth will set us free if we believe—free from this world's mindset and the world's religions of works to earn acceptance from gods or idols of this world. The One True God is not from this world. That is why Almighty God sent His Son to us, to save us from this world of sin and disobedience. We were born dead spiritually. That is why He came here; He came to set us free from Satan's lies. Satan is trying to get into our minds.

If you buy the lie, as Adam did, "Shame, you are not good enough, but if you work hard enough and it pleases God's will, He will save you," then Satan will win, and he will own you. But Jesus, the Son of God, came to save you. God the Father loves us, and He has chosen us before the creation of this world. Jesus came here to be a substitute for us. He has already paid the price for our sins in the spiritual realm. He has redeemed us and has set us free. This is why Christianity is the only way to be saved. Salvation is a gift of God. Ephesians 2:8–9: "For by grace you have been saved through faith; and that not of yourselves, it is a gift of God; not as a result of works, so that no one should boast." God's love is unconditional, and salvation cannot be earned; it is a gift. The question is, will you take it? Do you really believe who He is?

The difference between Christianity and all other religions is that Christians are saved through faith in Christ, not by their works. All other religions are based on faith, with emphasis on their works in order to be good enough to be accepted for what they did. Adam and Eve did not obey God's truth, and they lost their relationship with God.

Genesis 3:13–16, 20: "Then the Lord God said to the woman, 'What is this you have done?' And the woman said, 'The serpent deceived me, and I ate.' And the Lord God said to the serpent, 'Because you have done this, cursed are you more than all cattle. And I will put enmity between you and the woman; (between the seed of Satan and Eve) He shall bruise you on the head, and you (Satan) shall bruise Him in the heel.' To the woman He said, 'I will greatly multiply your pain in childbirth; in pain you shall bring forth children.'… Now the man called his wife's name Eve because she was the mother of all the living." Therefore, all descendants are born from Eve's seed and are born into this world with the consciousness of good and evil.

Our problem is, we were born without knowledge and the truth and wisdom of God. We do not have a relationship with our Father God. How can I find this knowledge? And God said, "It is written." The Bible is the living Word and the truth of God. How can this be? This book was written through inspired men in this world. The Bible was authored by forty writers, sixty-seven men, and edited by many more over fifteen hundred years. The ultimate test of this book is: do you believe that the Bible is the living Word and the truth? The answer is all about your faith; do you believe Jesus when He says in John 14:6, "I am the way, and the truth, and the life; no one comes to the Father but through Me"?

In the Gospels of Christ, He asked many times, "Do you believe I am who I am?" John 6:35–40: "Jesus said to them, 'I am the bread of life; he who comes to Me will not hunger, and he who believes in Me will never thirst. But I said to you, that you have seen Me and yet do not believe. All that the Father gives Me will come to Me, and the one who comes to Me I will certainly not cast out. For I have come down from heaven, not to do My own will but the will of Him who sent Me. And this is the will of Him who sent Me, that of all that He has given Me I lose nothing, but raise it up on the last day. For this is the will of My Father, that everyone who beholds the Son and believes in Him will have eternal life. And I Myself will raise him up on the last day.'"

In the Gospel of John, chapter 11, a dear friend of Jesus, Lazarus, was asleep (died), and Jesus said, "I will go, so that I may awaken him out of sleep." Notice what Jesus said: "I will awaken him." When they arrived at Lazarus's tomb, he had been dead for four days. Jesus said, in front of many people, including some Pharisees, "Take away the stone." And Jesus said in John 11:25, "I am the resurrection and the life; he who believes in Me will live even if he dies. And everyone who lives and believes in Me will never die. Do you believe this?"

John 11:24: "Then Jesus said with a loud voice, 'Lazarus, come forth.'" And they all saw, and many believed, except some of the Pharisees. At the council of the Pharisees, they decided to kill both Jesus and Lazarus.

This is the problem: the people of this world and the religions of this world have been deceived. They are in a state of denial or ignorance of the truth, and they are lost in this war over their souls. How can this be? The answer is, open your eyes and let them see the truth. And open your ears and let them hear the truth. Then the light of God will shine, and the way will be enlightened, and your feet will go along the right paths as you grow in your faith.

This is what Jesus said after the resurrection: "I will send to you the Comforter, the Holy Spirit. And He will lead you into His path, and you will learn the truth, the wisdom, and the knowledge from His Word." The Holy Spirit came here with a promise. Ephesians 1:13: "In Him, you also, after listening to the message of truth, the gospel of your salvation—having also believed, you were sealed in Him with the Holy Spirit of promise."

This is a note from the Ryrie Study Bible: Having also believed, this time of sealing coincides with the time of believing, sealed with the Holy Spirit. A seal indicates possession and security. The presence of the Holy Spirit, the seal, is the believer's guarantee of the security of his salvation.

After you have read my story, my hope is that you can see, hear, and understand some of the things I have learned in my life and from my poem. How can this be? It just is. What is faith? Hebrews 11:1–3: "Now faith is the assurance of things hoped for, the conviction of things not seen. For by it the men of old gained approval. By faith we understand that the worlds were prepared by the word of God, so that what is seen was not made out of things which are visible."

And Paul says in Romans 1:17–20, "For in it (the gospel) the righteousness of God is revealed from faith to faith; as it is written, 'But the righteous man shall live by faith.' For the wrath of God is revealed from heaven against all ungodliness and unrighteousness of men, who suppress the truth in unrighteousness, because that which is known about God is evident within them, for God has made it evident to them. For the invisible things of Him from the creation of this world, His eternal power and divine nature, are clearly seen, being understood by the things that are made, so that they are without excuse."

So this is what I learned. I was born spiritually dead. I was ignorant of God's truth. I was born with a consciousness of good and evil, right and wrong, but I was ignorant and in denial. Fools become wise, and wise become fools. In the end, I choose to become a fool, and I ask for the Comforter to help and lead me in my hope to be a son of God. And this is what I heard:

What Is Truth

According to "A Synopsis of Bible Doctrines" by Charles Ryrie in *Ryrie Study Bible, truth* means "agreement to and consistency with all that is represented by God Himself," God's view.

In my story and my poem, I found out this world is divided. There are basically three ways of thinking. One way is about performance; you have to be better than other people. A second way is to shame others so you will be better and you will get what you want. The third way is denial: "Just leave me alone. I will take care of myself." This is the world's view.

God's view is Jesus Christ. John 1:1–4: "In the beginning was the Word, and the Word was with God, and the Word was God. He was in the beginning with God. All things came into being through Him, and apart from Him nothing came into being that has come into being. In Him was life, and life was the light of men." And Jesus's name was Grace and Truth, according to the apostle John.

However, the church of Christ is divided also. Some of the churches believe God's Word is true; our job is to believe and choose Jesus as our Savior and Lord. Other churches are hybrids consisting of the Bible plus the secular world mindset, believing that it is good enough to be saved by your works. Or maybe some think they will be saved by His grace even though they do not believe in His Word, the Scriptures. He is the Word.

About ten years ago, I had a conversation with a person about what is truth. After a while, we disagreed about something. So he said, "Then we will just have to agree to disagree." I said, "No, I will not agree to that. I disagree to agree with you." Who was right? Later, I thought about it and decided we were both correct. The world's view is, "I am okay, are you okay?" God's view is, "No, I am not okay with that. My Word is Jesus, and He is true."

In the Bible, God teaches about double-minded people. They can see something in two different ways. James 1:8 says, "Being a double-minded man, unstable in all his ways." Also in James 1:22, "But prove yourselves doers of the Word, and not merely hearers who delude themselves." And Paul says in Romans 7:15, "For what I am doing, I do not understand; for I am not practicing what I would like to do, but I am doing the very thing I hate."

Romans 7:25: "Thanks be to God through Jesus Christ our Lord! So then, on the one hand I myself with my mind am serving the law of God, but on the other, my flesh (world's view), the law of sin." How can this be?

I believe we are all born in this world with free will, and we are here to be tested and to choose what we believe. I hope and pray you choose the truth. Do not be deceived. The war is in the mind. Your job is to choose: truth versus deceit and untruths.

If you are a spiritual person, then your religion will have to deal with the local laws and your religion's laws also. Either way, your behavior will be tested in your culture. Everyone believes in something, whether they are an atheist, an agnostic, or a member of a religion.

In the world view, whatever you believe, whatever you do, and who you are in this world is all your own effort, whether you are a member of a religion or not. It is all about you and your behaviors. You will be judged by the law; truth and lies; performance versus shame. Even some people who claim to be Christian will be judged the same way.

But a true Christian will see from God's eyes. God's view is *now* (His time). We were born into a mindset of the world's view. We are born dead to a relationship with our Creator. But He created a way back for us. He sent His Son, Jesus Christ, our Savior, to set us free from our behaviors. Jesus took all our sins, including bad behaviors, to the cross. He paid the price for our sins, and He set us free; now we do have a way back to God through Jesus. He said, "I Am the way."

The world mindset, our effort to do and to get, tells us that we are not good enough, that we need to be better in this world's eyes. Satan's lies have the power to shame and control us.

Should we do good works in this world? Yes, of course, but it should be done in the right way. Jesus said, "Love God, and love your neighbor as yourself." If you do this, then you will fulfill the whole law. In God's way, we cannot earn anything from these worldly efforts; we can only receive a free gift from the Father's love for our salvation. If we do works in this world that are prompted by the Holy Spirit, there will be rewards in heaven for that. But our salvation, as believers, is assured. You cannot "earn" salvation. This is the difference between Christianity and all other religions and this world. Salvation is a free gift, unmerited and unearned, from God. If you try to earn or work for something, that is a wage. Grace plus works does not work for your salvation. Grace and faith are a gift through the Holy Spirit.

Ephesians 1:13: "In Him, you also, after listening to the message of truth, the gospel of your salvation—having also believed, you were sealed in Him with the Holy Spirit of promise."

Change your mind and believe in His name, Jesus Christ, and you will be saved eternally.

Paul talks about the mind. Romans 12:2–3: "And do not be conformed to this world, but be transformed in the renewing of your mind, so that you may prove what the will of God is, that which is good and acceptable and perfect."

This reminded me of John 3:3: "Truly, truly, I say to you, unless one is born again, he cannot see the kingdom of God."

Creation

God created the world in six days, and on the seventh day, He rested. Genesis 2:1–3: "And the heavens and the earth were finished (completed) and all the host of them. And God blessed the seventh day, and hallowed it (sanctified = set apart)." These are the generations of the heaven and earth when they were created on the day that Jehovah God made the heavens and earth. Everything was good, and man had been given free will. He was dependent and had a fellowship and relationship with God.

But Adam sinned and lost his relationship with God.

I learned that Jesus came here to seek and save the lost. How can this be? Because there was and is an adversary, Satan, who prowls around the earth seeking whom he can devour rather than save. This is why I was born into a world of sin. This is Satan's game: to lie, and tell that you are not good enough. It is called the circle of shame.

Creation of the World

Genesis 2:16–17: "And Jehovah God commanded the man, saying, of every tree of the garden thou mayest freely eat but of the tree of the knowledge of good and evil, thou shalt not eat of it: for in the day that thou eat thereof thou shalt surely die."

Man had a choice: Believe God's truth and live or eat the fruit of Satan's lie and die.

Genesis 2:25: "And they were both naked, the man and his wife, and were not ashamed."

"Naked" = totally in dependence on God and all things He created, totally in relationship with their Father.

"They were not ashamed" = innocence, without shame and sin.

Genesis 3:1: "Now the <u>serpent</u> was more subtle than any beast of the field which Jehovah God had made. And he said unto the woman, Yea, hath God said, Ye shall not eat of any tree of the garden?"

Created doubt = can I achieve more than I already have?

Genesis 3:2–4: "And the woman said unto the serpent, Of the fruit of the trees of the garden we may eat; but of the fruit of the tree which is in the midst of the garden, God hath said, Ye shall not eat of it, neither shall ye touch it, lest ye die. And the serpent said unto the woman, Ye surely shall not die!"

Doubt entered her mind.

Genesis 3:5: "For God doth know that in the day ye eat thereof, then your eyes shall be opened, and ye shall be as God, knowing good and evil."

This is the lie of Satan. Doubt turns to unbelief which turns to sin.

From the beginning until now = the same lie to all people.

Genesis 3:6: "And when the woman saw that the tree was good for food, and that it was a delight to the eyes, and that the tree was to be desired to make one wise, she took of the fruit thereof, and did eat; and she gave also unto her husband with her, and he did eat."

When the woman saw the chance to become wise, she bought the lie. They were not good enough as they were. You are lacking but if you eat the fruit, you will be more than you already are. Trying to become more and to become wise, you become fools.

Genesis 3:7: "And the eyes of them both were opened, and they knew that they were naked; and they sewed fig-leaves together, and made themselves aprons."

Notice: The difference between being dependent on God and being on their own: independence brings shame and awareness of sin.

Genesis 3:8–10: "And they heard the sound of Jehovah God walking in the garden in the cool of the day: and the man and his wife hid themselves from the presence of Jehovah God amongst the trees of the garden. And Jehovah God called to the man "where are you" and the man said, "I heard Thy voice in the garden, and I was afraid, because I was naked".

Fear of lacking, not being complete, or not good enough = leads to disobedience (Genesis 3:6)

Unbelief (Genesis 3:4) = leads to

Disobedience = leads to

Shame and awareness of sin (Genesis 3:10) = leads to

Fear, and the cycle begins again.

Their sin was more than merely eating the forbidden fruit: it was disobeying the revealed word of God, believing the lie of Satan, and placing their own wills above God's. Sin, with all its dreadful consequences, now entered the human race.

Adam and Eve tried to gain from their own self-effort what they already had = everything, all for free, and it was good.

The lie of Satan from the beginning to now is his *game of shame!* It is the biggest tool of Satan, to deceive us to turn from belief to unbelief = sin.

Notice the difference from Old Testament Genesis 2:25 to Genesis 3:10 to New Testament James 1:14–17:

Genesis 2:25 = they were dependent, and in relationship with God

Genesis 3:10 = now independent, and out of relationship with God

James 1:14–16 = our choice, independence or dependence on God

James 1:14: "but each one is tempted, when he is carried away and enticed by his own lust."

James 1:15: "Then the lust, when it hath conceived, beareth sin: and the sin, when it is full-grown, bringeth forth death."

James 1:16: "Be not deceived, my beloved brethren."

James 1:17: "Every good gift and every perfect gift is from above, coming down from the Father of lights, with whom can be no variation, neither shadow that is cast by turning."

But God's answer is from the cross = our redeemer lives (Job: 19:25)

It's the same lie from Adam's sin until Satan's lies now.
Do not be deceived.

This diagram below is how I envision shame: as a circle.

Old Testament from Genesis	New Testament from James

God Had a Plan of Stopping This Circle of Shame

Genesis 3:15: "To the serpent God said "and I will put enmity between thee and the woman, and between thy seed [Satan] and her seed [Jesus]: he shall bruise thee on thy head, and thou shalt bruise him on his heel."

Genesis 3:17–19: "Then to Adam He said, 'Because you have listened to the voice of your wife, and eaten from the tree about which I commanded you saying, you shall not eat from it; Cursed is the ground because of you; In toil you shall eat of it all the days of your life, Both the thorns and thistles it shall grow for you: And you shall eat the plants of the field; by the sweat of your face you shall eat bread till you return to the ground. Because from it you were taken: for you are dust, and to dust you shall return."

Genesis 3:24: "So He drove the man out; and at the east of the garden of Eden He stationed the cherubim and the flaming sword which turned every direction to guard the way to the tree of life."

What happened to Adam and Eve? They did not believe. Therefore, they lost eternal life and they had to die in this world. They were created in this world in the image of God, and they were made complete. They were given eternal life. But they were deceived by Satan's lie of "not good enough." They lost their relationship with God. They had free will to choose to be dependent on Him or to be independent by their own effort. There were two different kinds of trees in the garden. One kind they could eat of it. The second tree they were told not to eat of it or they would surely die. This was the tree of life and the knowledge of good and evil. Eat it and you will die and return back to the dust.

This is why Jesus came here, to save us. He is The Redeemer for our sins of unbelief. He gave us time to choose and to get back into a relationship of dependence on God. Because of Adam's sin, we are born now into this world and are independent, on our own effort. We are alive in this world, Satan's world, and we are born dead to a relationship with God, our Creator. We are born with a body, a soul, and a spirit. But like Adam our spirit is dead and eternal life is gone. We have no relationship with God now. Our body and our spirit will return to the dust. But when God breathed into Adam's body, he received an eternal soul forever. The question is where will it go? Remember when Jesus said, "Born of the flesh is flesh and born of the Spirit is spirit?" (Ephesians 3:6). How can this be? Have you heard this saying before, "Born once dies twice, born twice dies once"?

John 3:3–6: "Truly, truly, I say to you unless one is born again, he cannot see the kingdom of God. Nicodemus said to Him [Jesus], How can a man be born when he is old? He cannot enter a second time into his mother's womb and be born, can he? Truly, truly I say to you, unless is born of water and the Spirit he cannot enter unto the kingdom of God. That which is born of the flesh is flesh [world view] and that which is born of the Spirit is spirit."

John 3:15 (KJV): "That whoever believeth in Him should not perish but have eternal life."

Ephesians 1:13: "In Him, you also, after listening to the message of truth, the gospel of your salvation having also believed you were sealed in Him with the Holy Spirit of promise."

It is finished.

Receipts for taxes found in the papyri have written across them a single Greek word, which means "paid in full." The price for our redemption from sin was paid in full by the Lord's death.

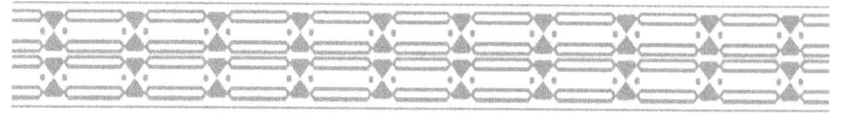

Know It: Knowledge

Salvation Is Your Choice

From my story:

I was outside, shoveling snow during February of 1982, when I collapsed in defeat. Finally, the heavy thoughts of not measuring up overwhelmed me. I violently gathered snow then hurled it as hard as I could against the garage door in frustration. It was my only response to the harassing thoughts in my head. My strength was finished, and I was completely bare of any power to overcome the problems surrounding me. I fell into the snow and stared into the cold winter sky. I thought of the day in Utah when I turned my back on God for a lonely, sinking ship of self. This gray Minnesota day was familiar, but different: familiar because I had fallen short once again, but different because I had finally realized that no answer, or way out, lay within any part of my struggling self. So I rose from the snow and uncorked my ears, giving their attention to the sound of God. After a while, I started to see my whole life: golf and sports were my source, and God had been my resource. But now, I had fallen so low that I was willing to abandon my own efforts and give control back to God. God has the right to all control, but He never demands it.

So I said, "If You are really here, my golf will be a resource and *You* will be my source." My path back to God was a subtle journey of discovering a gift He had given to me and to the entire world before the dawn of creation; the secret is my will versus God's will.

From my poem:
>Free—from the wages of sin
>Free—from the grasp of shame
>Free—from death within
>By the power of His name

The Gospel
Grace, Truth, and Time

And I, brethren, when I came unto you, came not with excellency of speech or of wisdom, proclaiming to you the testimony of God. For I determined not to know anything among you, except Jesus Christ, and Him crucified. And I was with you in weakness and in fear and in much trembling. And my speech and my preaching were not in persuasive words of wisdom, but in demonstration of the Spirit and of power, that your faith should not stand in the wisdom of men, but in the power of God. (1 Corinthians 2:1–5)

After my stroke in 1999, I was someone who could barely speak or write a sentence. On top of that, my heart was failing. I really had no vision for the future. So I found my poem, and I decided that I was going to find out what it meant.

A friend of mine came by and brought me a leftover computer. Oh God, I couldn't write, I could barely speak, and now a computer. Good luck! But quickly I repented and said, "Lord, please help me, I want to understand this poem." By the grace of God, my mind was still clear, and I could hear and read. I learned how to use a computer, and I used an outline program. I did not have the ability to create a sentence or a paragraph, but I had an icon for spell-check. So I attacked this poem, word by word and sentence by sentence. I used the concordance for words, and I studied every word and sentence. I kept in mind how to use the tools of hermeneutics—how to study the Bible. Now in 2000, I knew why He gave me my poem. He was not finished yet with my time. The poem was the key, His key, to helping me regain my ability to speak.

It was hard. I was like a kid with my first bike. But slowly I started to learn. Amazingly, I started to see what I had—it was amazing grace all over again. It just abounds even more. This is a progressive gospel through time and grace. Five years later, in 2005, I had 152 pages of pictures, scriptures, and commentaries with help from my *Ryrie Study Bible*.

In 1982, when I decided to give up my golf god, I went to the Open Door and found a real God: Jesus Christ. I learned. In John 14:6, Jesus says, "I am the way, the truth, and the life; no one comes to the Father but through Me." This is the truth that I learned.

When I was young, I knew about Jesus, but I did not know Him. When I came to the Open Door, I did not have any religious baggage. So I was lucky! I was just a puppy, but I was blessed to run around with the big dogs. I was taught well at the Open Door. As for the gift of prophecy, one thing I do know: it is a gift of God's grace. And my ability to speak and write and understand the poem has increased tremendously over time.

First Corinthians 14:1, 3: "Pursue love, yet desire earnestly spiritual gifts, but especially that you may prophesy… But one who prophesies speaks to men for edification and exhortation and consolation."

I will not prophesy, that is, not to speak in the foreknowledge of time. But I am conformable with things that I know—I know who I Am. I was taught well through the church of the Open Door from 1982 to 1990. Pastor Dave Johnson showed me not to just read the Bible but to study it for myself. He taught hermeneutics, to study the Bible in the context of His Word, culture, location, language, and time! I adopted this approach with what I call the six W's: who, what, why, when, where, will.

In addition, Jeff VanVonderen was also part of the church of the Open Door: a pastor, a counselor, a strange dude. I say that with great respect. Jesus was not a normal person either. Jesus is Jehovah-Yahweh: "I Am Lord." Dave, Jeff, I, or anyone who is in the Body of Christ are one with Christ, but we are also individually unique.

The year 1990 was a time for change, mostly due to my job. I could not stay. The Golf Country Club had a corporate mindset. Performance was everything; performance, works, and self-identification, as well as failure, poor esteem, and shame. This is not unique to conservatives, liberals, or whoever. From my perspective, this is a world mindset. But when I went to the Open Door in 1982, I learned the *gospel of grace and faith.* I learned who I am.

From Dave Johnson, 2 Corinthians 5:17: "Therefore if anyone is in Christ, he is a new creature; the old things passed away; behold, new things have come." I was done with the old person; now I walk as a new person. And from Jeff, Romans 1:16–17, "For I am not ashamed of the gospel, for it is the power of God for salvation to everyone who believes, to the Jew first and also to the Greek. For in it the righteousness of God is revealed from faith to faith; as it is written, But the righteous man shall live by faith." I learned that I am a new man; the old man died to fear of shame and sin.

The Open Door was a unique place. The door was a revolving door; we used to call the Open Door a hospital because a person could come in sick with shame or low esteem and go out healed in body, soul, and spirit by God's grace and truth. Being part of this church was a time of learning and rest. Matthew 11:28: "Come to Me, all who are weary and heavy laden, and I will give you rest." During this time, the church grew from 150 to 5,000 people.

In 1990, my family and I were ready to leave. I was not sad to leave my job or the culture where I was, but I was very sad to leave the Open Door and the fellowship I experienced there. Thank God for the Open Door. I was taught well; I learned the truth, the real gospel, and the truth of Christ, and His truth set me free. Thank you, Jesus, that I am with You and I am secure in You.

But when my family and I left our church and moved to another place, I was in shock. How can this be? I didn't know then how unique the Open Door church was, or that I would not find another church like it. Why? Because many churches teach a combination of Spirit and works. Is there a problem with works?

John 10:25–28: "Jesus answered them, I told you, and you do not believe; the works that I do in My Father's name, these testify of Me. But you do not believe because you are not of My sheep. My sheep hear My voice, and I know them, and they follow Me. And I give eternal life to them, and they will never perish; and no one will snatch them out of My hand." *Notice* the context here that Jesus is speaking to the multitude of people, but also especially to the Pharisees, leaders of the temple.

And Paul verifies this in 1 Corinthians 15:10–11: "But by the grace of God I am what I am, and His grace toward me did not prove in vain; but I labored even more than all of them, yet not I, but the grace of God with me. Whether then it was I or they, so we preach, and so you believed." I do believe and teach the same gospel.

Galatians 1:6–10: "I am amazed that you are so quickly deserting Him who called you by the grace of Christ, for a different gospel; which is really not another; only there are some who are disturbing you and want to distort the gospel of Christ. But even if we, or an angel from heaven, should preach to you a gospel contrary to what we have preached to you, he is to be accursed."

Quickly, I found why Paul was frustrated and angry when he said, "You foolish Galatians, who has bewitched you" (Galatians 3:1). The problem was that if righteousness comes through works of the Law, then the grace of God is nullified. Paul said in Galatians 2:21, "I do not nullify the grace of God; for if righteousness comes through the Law, then Christ died needlessly." And according to my annotated Bible, "to return to law and negate the necessity of the death of Christ was to act bewitched. Works of the Law did not give them the Holy Spirit" (*Ryrie Study Bible*). The people were deceived.

The sequence of Paul's verses is as follows:

> Galatians 3:1–5: "You foolish Galatians,
>   who has bewitched you, before whose eyes Jesus Christ
> was publicly portrayed as crucified?
> This is the only thing I want to find out from
>   you: did you receive
>   the Spirit by works of the Law or
>   by hearing with faith?
> Are you so foolish? Having begun by the Spirit
>   are you now being perfected by the flesh (works)?
> Did you suffer so many things in vain,
>   if indeed it was in vain
> So then, does He who provides you with the
>   *Spirit* (Holy Spirit)
>   and works miracles among you,
>   do it by the works of the Law (Old Testament) or
>   by hearing with faith." (New Testament)

I have a question: Have you been deceived? Do you believe, like the Galatians, that salvation depends on works?

Salvation

First, believe and seek the truth from Jesus. Matthew 6:33: "*But seek first His kingdom and His righteousness and all these things will be added to you.*" I would like to go through a few scriptures about salvation. These are classic scriptures for any true Christian who believes in and knows the Gospel of Jesus. Romans 10:9–10 says "that if you confess with your mouth Jesus as Lord, and believe in your heart that

God raised Him from the dead, you will be saved; for with the heart a person believes, resulting in righteousness, and with the mouth to confess, resulting in salvation."

Romans 5:12: "Therefore, as through one man sin entered into the world, and death through sin and so, death passed unto all men, because all sinned."

Here in Romans 3:21–25, Paul teaches that through Adam's sin, all men have received the universality of sin. Sin = death. "For all have sinned and fall short of the glory of God." The point here is to be in sin = death to a relationship with Abba Father God.

I will quote Paul from Romans 3:10–20:

> As it is written, there is none righteous, not even one; there is none who understands, there is none who seeks for God; all have turned aside, together they have become useless; there is none who does good; there is not even one; their throat is an open grave; with their tongues they keep deceiving, the poison of asps is under their lips; whose mouth is full of cursing and bitterness; their feet are swift to shed blood, destruction and misery are in their paths; and the path of peace they have not known, there is no fear of God before their eyes. Because by the works of Law no flesh will be justified in His sight; for through the Law comes the knowledge of sin.

However; the Good News is the Gospel of Grace is free *to all who believe.*

One of my favorite scriptures is Ephesians 2:1–10 in which Paul lays out the whole plan of salvation: "8 For by grace you have been saved through faith: and that not of yourself, it is a gift of God; 9 not as a result of works, so that no one may boast."

We were born dead in sin. The worldview is from Satan's lies, to lead us into disobedience or unbelief in God. Why? We were born spiritually dead.

We were dead. Ephesians: 2:1 "And you were dead in your trespasses and sins."

After Adam and Eve all people were born naturally (John 3:6), they were born in Adam's sin. Their spirits were empty and dead in relationship to God (Genesis 3:6–7; Romans 3:10–12, 5:12).

Ephesians 2:2: "in which you formerly walked according to the course of this world, according to the prince of the air [Satan], of the spirit that is now working in the sons of disobedience."

People are walking spiritually dead, with no relationship with Jehovah, our Creator, our Lord.

Ephesians 2:3: "Among them we too all formerly lived in the lusts of our flesh, indulging the desires of the flesh and of the mind, and were by nature children of wrath, even as the rest."

But in Ephesians 2:4: "God, being rich in mercy, for his great love wherewith he loved us."

"God being rich in love" = He loved us even though we were dead (no life in us). *But God can make us alive through Christ* if we choose Him.

"Mercy" = We did not receive what we deserved.

"Grace" = We did receive what was unmerited and undeserved, favor, which was freely bestowed.

Ephesians 2:5: "even when we were dead in our transgressions, made us alive together with Christ [by grace you have been saved]."

We were dead in our sins, but He made us alive in Christ. By grace, you have been saved (Acts 15:11, Romans 3:24, Ephesians 2:8–9).

See the poem "Behold."

Ephesians 2:6: "and raised us up with Him, and made us to sit with Him in the heavenly places, in Christ Jesus."

Places in the Bible when God (Jesus, Jehovah) told us when His work was finished, complete, accomplished, done, fulfilled totally.

"So, he sat down at the right hand of God" (Hebrews 10:12), and He will raise us up with Him.

Ephesians 2:7: "that in the ages to come He might show the exceeding riches of his grace in kindness toward us in Christ Jesus."

Ages (in Greek) = periods of time

"By God's time" = to show the exceeding riches of his grace

Ephesians 2:8: "for by grace have ye been saved through faith; and that not of yourselves, it is the gift of God."

Grace = the unmerited and undeserved gift of God for salvation to all who believe. It never has anything to do with ourselves.

Grace = a gift = free, without cost. It cannot be earned, or it would not be a gift but a wage. For the wages of sin is death, but the free gift of God is eternal life.

Faith = knowledge of the gospel (Romans 10:14–17).

Acknowledge the truth of the gospel, personal reception of the Savior

People cannot work for their salvation (Romans 3:28; Titus 3:5)

No man should glory (1 Corinthians 1:29)

Ephesians 2:9: "not of works, that no one may boast."

But we are his workmanship.

Ephesians 2:10: "For we are his workmanship, created in Christ Jesus for good works, which God prepared beforehand that we should walk in them."

We are His workmanship = in us, not by us. Created in Christ Jesus = not of our own works. But we can, and should, do good works, which God prepared beforehand (in His time).

"I was lost but now I have been found." This is the main theme of this teaching from God's Word and from my poem. This is the Gospel of Grace. Salvation is a gift if you are willing to ask for it. It is your choice.

Or do you want to do it through your works? Paul talks about this in 1 Corinthians:1–3, that fools became wise and the wise become fools, and the difference between salvation and works for rewards.

Back to Ephesians 2:10: "For we are His workmanship, created in Christ Jesus for good works, which God prepared beforehand so that we should walk in them." Yes, we are chosen to walk in His works. But beware, works must be works through Him. "Enter the narrow gate; for the gate is wide and the way is broad that leads to destruction, and there are many who enter through it. For the gate is small and the way is narrow that leads to life, and there are few who find it" beware of false prophets (Matthew 7:13–14). If you think you can enter God's Kingdom through your works, beware; your works will count for a reward but they will not count toward salvation. (See 1 Corinthians 3:10–22, pages 31–32). Salvation is free.

Ephesians 1:11–13 is about inheritance and the Holy Spirit. Salvation is a gift to the believer and he receives an inheritance in Jesus. And we were made His inheritance. (We are Christ's inheritance as he is ours.) Notice here, *"once you believed you were sealed in Him with the Holy Spirit of promise."* (You are born again, saved, and received; Jesus promised the Comforter at the cross.) It is finished, past tense, and cannot be changed.

For me, John 3:16 and Romans 1:17 are the two of the most important scriptures concerning salvation.

John 3:16 states, "For God so loved the world, that He gave His only begotten Son, that whoever believes in Him should not perish, but have eternal life."

Romans 1:17: "For in it is the righteousness of God as revealed from faith to faith; as it is written, But the righteous man shall live by faith." I suggest studying and meditating on these two.

Being on the Right Side

His righteousness or our righteousness
Faith righteousness versus works righteousness

Philippians 3:9: "And I may be found in him, not having a righteousness of mine own, even that which is of the Law, but that which is through faith in Christ, the *righteousness which is from God by faith.*"
Study Romans 3:21–5:21; meditate on this truth.

Faith Righteousness (God's view)	Works Righteousness (Worldview)
A. Grow from the inside out	Grow from the outside in
B. Grace	Works or law
C. Grace is not liberalism	Legalism is not grace
D. Objective to = who you are	Subjective to = what you do
E. Who you are. Learn and use what you already have.	What you do = try to gain more and more than what you already have.
F. Adam was in dependence but sinned. Then we all became independent by our own will.	Adam was in dependence but sinned. Then we all became independent by our own will.
G. In sin we were lost.	In sin we were lost.
H. By Grace we are saved through faith + nothing. Our salvation is finished, completed, at the cross.	We are saved by grace through faith + works to retain our salvation.
I. We have gone from independence back to dependence = on Him and His work.	We were independent and stay in independence = in our works.

J. Fear of God for a son of God = awe or reverence of God, our Father. He owns us now. He has Redeemed us and paid the price to get us back. I was lost but now I've been found. "And no one shall snatch them out of My hand" (John 10:28).	Fear = fear. If a person believes that they could lose their salvation, and that they are not good enough, they try, try, try, but this will not save anyone.

John 6:28: "They said therefore unto Him, what must we do, that we may work the works of God?"

John 6:29: "Jesus answered and said unto them, this is the work of God, that you *believe in Him* whom He hath sent."

First Corinthians 3:14–15: "If any man's work which he has built upon remains, he will receive a reward. If any man's work is burned up, he will suffer loss; but he himself will be saved (salvation), yet so as through fire." Some people believe a Christian can lose their salvation. It is clear here and throughout the scriptures you may lose a reward but no real Christian can lose their salvation. Being saved through Jesus you are His inheritance. And our inheritance is in Him.

John 10:27–29: "My sheep hear my voice, and I know them, and they follow me: and I give unto them eternal life; and they shall never perish, and no one shall snatch them out of my hand. My Father, who hath given them unto me, is greater than all; and no one is able to snatch them out of the Father's hand." Because we are in the Age of Grace, we are not bound in the Law (Romans 8:4, 13:8; Galatians 5:14; Matthew 5:17).

Romans 9:30: "What shall we say then? That the Gentiles, who followed not after righteousness, attained to righteousness, even the righteousness which is of faith."

Romans 10:3–4: "For being ignorant of God's righteousness, and seeking to establish their own, they did not subject themselves to the righteousness of God. For Christ is the end of the law unto righteousness to everyone that believes."

Christ is the termination of the Law. It could not provide righteousness based on merit, but Christ provides righteousness based on God's grace in response to faith.

Okay, I want to know the answer to this question: Can a true believer in Jesus Christ lose a free gift of salvation? God has given us free will. Do not confuse *works* with *salvation*.

First Corinthians 3:10–23:

(10) "According to the grace of God which was given to me, like a wise master builder I laid a foundation, and another is building on it. But each man must be careful how he builds upon it [by grace through faith)."

Paul has built a foundation through Jesus Christ. It is the Gospel of Grace. Be careful, make sure you know the right Gospel and not a different gospel.

(11) "For no man can lay a foundation other than the one which is laid, which is Jesus Christ."

(12) "Now if any man builds upon the foundation with gold, silver, precious stones, wood hay, straw."

Gold, silver and precious stones: these are everlasting works. Wood, hay and straw are also works but they are worthless.

(13) "Each man's work will become evident; for the day will show it because it is to be revealed with fire, and fire itself will test the quality of each man's work."

These works will be revealed at the judgment seat of Christ. These works will be tested by fire. It is not about the quantity of your works but the quality of your service.

(14) "If any man's work which he has built on it remains, he will receive a reward."

If your works go through the judgement seat and they are not destroyed you will receive a reward.

(15) "If any man's work is burned up, he will suffer loss; but he himself will be saved, yet so as through fire."

If your works are worthless, they will be burned up, destroyed, and you will not receive a reward, a crown. Good works are valuable to receive a crown for your effort. However, your rewards are worthless for your salvation, you cannot earn anything toward grace. If you add anything to grace, it would no longer be grace but works. Rewards are from your works. *Salvation is a gift by His grace, not of your works.*

> Galatians 2:21: "I do not nullify the grace of God, for if righteousness comes through the Law, then Christ died needlessly."

> Ephesians 2:8–9: "For by Grace you have been saved through faith: and that not of yourself, it is a gift of God. it is not a result *of your works*, so that no one can boast".

> Ephesians 1:13: "You were sealed in Him with the Holy Spirit of promise."

(16) "Do you not know that you are a temple of God and that the Spirit of God dwells in you?"

The foundation of your temple (you) was built on a foundation of Grace + faith + nothing = salvation.

> Romans 1:17: "The righteous man shall live by faith."

(17) "If any man destroys the temple of God, God will destroy him, for the temple of God is holy, and that is what you are."

Any man who contributes to collapse a local church, either a believer or a non-believer, will be severely disciplined.

(18) "Let no man deceive himself. If any man among you thinks that he is wise in this age [a period of time], he must become foolish so that he may become wise." The world regards God's wisdom as folly.

(19) "For the wisdom of this world is foolishness before God. For it is written, He is the one who catches the wise in their craftiness,"

(20) "and again, the Lord knows the reasoning of the wise, that they are useless."

The world has an upside-down theology.

(21) "So then let no one boast in men. For all things belong to you,"

(22) "whether Paul or Apollos or Cephas, or the world or life or death or things present or things to come; all things belong to you."

Your inheritance is in God's kingdom.

(23) "and you belong to Christ; and Christ belongs to God."

You are secure in Jesus Christ.

Doctrine of Salvation

From Charles Ryrie ThD, PhD. *Ryrie Study Bible*, "Doctrine of Salvation"

> Therefore, if anyone is in Christ, he is a new creature; the old things passed away; behold new things have come. Now all these things are from God, who reconciled us to himself through Christ and gave us the ministry of reconciliation. (2 Corinthians 5:17–18)

The meaning and blessings of Salvation.

Accomplishments of Christ's death.

Substitution for sin. Matthew 20:28, Mark 10:45

Redemption from sin. Matthew 13:44. Doctrine of redemption from the blood of Christ. Hebrews 9:12, Titus 2:14.

Reconciliation. 2 Corinthians 5:19.

Propitiation = to satisfy or appease God = a personal intervention of God in the affairs of mankind. Romans 3:25.

Judgment the sin nature Romans 6:1–6.

Brought the End of the Law. Rom 10:4, Col 2:14. This is the beginning of the New Testament. The importance here is *justification and sanctification*. This means that the death of Christ provided the way for justification by faith in Him alone. Romans 1:17: "For in it the righteousness of God is revealed from faith to faith; as it is written. *But the righteous man shall live by faith.*"

The ground of a believer is from justification, adoption, and sanctification.

Justification. Justification could never be based on our good works. For God requires perfect obedience, which is impossible for man. The means of justification is faith (Romans 3:22, 25, 28). Faith is never grounded on Justification; it is the means or channel through which *God's grace* can impute to the believing sinner the righteousness of Christ. When we believe, all that Christ is, God puts to our account; thus, we stand acquitted. Then God can justly announce the acquittal, and that pronouncement is justification.

Adoption Galatians 4:5–7 Sons of God.

Sanctification. The word sanctify means "to set apart." This contains three parts.

This is called *positional sanctification*; First, a believer has been set apart by his position in the family of God (Hebrews 10:10).

The second part is experiential *aspect of sanctification*. We have been set apart in our daily lives (1 Peter 1:16).

And the third part is when we see Christ and we will become as He is (1 John 3:1–3). This is *the ultimate or future sanctification* as we a waiting for the glorification with resurrection bodies (Ephesians 5:26–27).

Doctrine of man
Blessing of salvation
Blessing of Acceptance
Redeemed (Romans 3:24)
Reconciled (2 Corinthians 5:19–21)
Forgiven (Romans 3:25)
Delivered (Colossians 1:13)
Accepted (Ephesians 1:6)
Justified (Romans 3:24)
Glorified (Romans 8:30)
Blessing of position
Citizen of heaven (Philippians 3:2)

When I was copying notes out of Ryrie's doctrine about salvation, I had to stop and remind myself of what this was. "Beware of the dogs, beware of the evil workers, beware of the false circumcision (3) for we are true circumcision who worship in the Spirit of God and glory in Christ Jesus and put no confidence in the flesh." This is my opinion of why Ryrie put this scripture here. Paul is very well aware that false teachers are not teaching Paul's Gospel of Grace, faith to faith alone. Romans 11:6: "But if it is by grace, it is no longer on the basis of works, otherwise grace is no longer grace." I believe *beware* is a warning. Don't be deceived.

When Jesus speaks to the multitudes He always asks, "Do you believe this?" So, I will ask you the same thing: do you believe this? Or do you think it is possible for a person to lose their salvation?

In order to lose one's salvation, all these works of God would have to be undone, and the Bible nowhere even hints that this is possible.

The condition: Salvation is conditioned solely on faith in Jesus Christ. Nearly two hundred times *faith* or *belief* is stated as the single condition in the New Testament John 1:12 or Acts 16:31. That faith must be placed in Christ as one's substitute for the Savior from sin, it is not easy to believe someone whom you have never seen about the most important matter of eternal destiny, but this is the only way to be saved.

The law of the Old and the New Testaments leads us to Christ

The law of Moses is like a mirror to show us who we are under the law. Romans 3.20: "Because the works of the Law there shall no flesh be justified in His sight: for through the law comes the knowledge of sin."

Galatians 3:24: "So that the law has become our <u>tutor</u> to bring us unto Christ, that we might be justified by faith."

Galatians 3:25: "But now that has come, we are no longer under a tutor."

We no longer need a teacher under the Mosaic Law. The law teaches us from the beginning until now that Adam and Eve had free will but they sinned. God gave them a blessing and a curse. The curse was they sinned and they would die. The blessing was the Redeemer came to set us free of our sins. Jesus was the seed of Eve, the mother of life.

When Noah built the ark, the whole earth was corrupted in sin, and all but eight died in the flood. Noah's family was saved through the ark (they believed and they were blessed). They continued the family line of "the Seed" and worshipped through the blood of the covenant at that time.

Abraham was blessed in God's covenants. Abraham created a new race and a new nation. He believed and received righteousness by grace. Circumcision as worship began with Abraham.

Moses led the nation of Israel under the law, the priesthood (Levites) and the tabernacle, civil law, and the Ten Commandments of the Law.

However, Now in the New Testament

Romans 3:20: "because by the works of the Law shall no flesh be justified in His sight; for through the law cometh the knowledge of sin."

Romans 3:23: "for all have sinned, and fall short of the glory of God."

But now, after the cross, we are not under the law but under grace.

Romans 8:1: "There is therefore *now no condemnation* to those who are in Christ Jesus."

Now = now. The word *now* is present tense. The word cannot be changed. Absolutely, a legal verdict cannot be changed. God never condemns us. We need to learn that we should not condemn ourselves or others.

Romans 8:2–4: "For the law of the Spirit of life in Christ Jesus has set you free from the law of sin and of death. For what the Law could not do, in that it was weak through the flesh, God did: sending His own Son in the likeness of sinful flesh and as an offering for sin, He condemned sin in the flesh: that the ordinance of the law might be fulfilled in us, who walk not after the flesh, but after the Spirit."

The Holy Spirit Leads us to become sons of God

Galatians 3:26: "For ye are all sons of God, through faith, in Christ Jesus."

Leads us to be heirs according to the promise

Galatians 3:29: "And if ye are Christ's, then are ye Abraham's seed, heirs according to promise."

We are all heirs with all who believed in Christ, according to the promise of Abraham. There are guardians and stewards to lead us to Christ and we will be children of God.

Leads us out of bondage of the Law

Galatians 4:4: *"but when the fulness of the time came, God sent forth his Son, born of a woman, born under the Law."* We were all born under the bondage of the Law, even Jesus was born under the Law. The law leads us to the Redeemer (Jesus), and we are adopted as His children.

Galatians 4:5: "that he might redeem them that were under the law, that we might receive the adoption as sons."

Galatians 4:6: "And because ye are sons, God sent forth the <u>Spirit of his Son into our hearts,</u> crying, Abba, Father."

Leads us to receive the Holy Spirit

Because we are his sons, we have a new heart. We were dead = lost. We had no life in us because our hearts, our spirits, were dead to God. But he gave us a new heart and a New Spirit [Holy Spirit] and now we are in THE NEW COVENANT.

Hebrews 10:16–18: "This is the new covenant that I will make with them after those days, says the Lord. I will put My laws upon their heart and on their mind and I will write them. He then says, and their sins and their lawless deeds I will remember no more. Now where there is forgiveness of these things, there is no longer *any* offering for sin."

Leads us as heirs of the kingdom

Galatians 4:6–7: "So that thou art no longer a bondservant, but a son; and if a son, then an heir through God, are heirs of his will, because he died for our sins, and we are his sons and we received the inheritance in the kingdom." We are citizens of the kingdom. We are aliens, not of this world.

Second Corinthians 5:17: "you are a new creature; the old things passed away; behold, new things have come."

Who and what are we in this world?

Our needs are met in Christ. We need to know that human beings have basic needs to be met in order to be a healthy person:

To be loved and accepted.

To feel valuable, capable, and worthwhile and know that we are not alone.

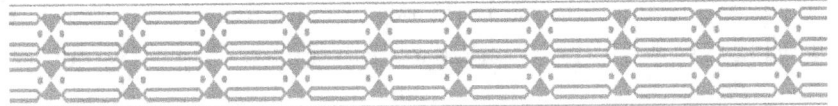

Believe It

Faith

It is a time to change. Grace and truth.
Jesus is the way.

From my story:

Grace was beyond my understanding. Everything that I had ever hoped and dreamed of had already been given to me through the man, Jesus Christ. His gift was free. He required no work from my hands. I realized that Jesus had given me a receipt and not an invoice, contrary to the way I had lived up until that point in time.

I didn't have to work to be better anymore.

I no longer bought into the lie that I had to do something or act in a certain way to receive something that I was lacking. Adam was perfectly like God and needed nothing before he ate the fruit. I finally realized that I didn't need to eat any more fruit to become somebody I already was in Jesus Christ.

I had been set free in my mind to know the gift that God had released through Jesus's death and resurrection on the cross. I mulled over Romans 11:6, and my life grew in satisfaction for the love of God: "But if it is by grace, it is no longer on the basis of works, otherwise, grace is no longer grace."

I finally found out that in the beginning, I knew about Jesus but now I know Him. To know Him is to see the mindset of men: worldview versus God's view.

From my poem:

> Behold the Lord Thy God
> You oh Ancient of Days
> Sovereign from the start
> You mold us in your ways
> You told me not to fear
> To get strength from you on High
> Before—I listened with my ear
> But now—I see you with my eye
>
> Understand the parables of God's kingdom
>
> Remember the beginning of my story?
> How can this be?
> This story is a gift.
> He who has eyes let him see,
> He who has ears let him hear

Do you have a foundation that is built on truth? Can you trust your feelings, emotions, and truth? We have free will; we can choose what we believe. When I was young, I learned about God, but I never really knew him but the seed of truth was still there. But in college, I got frustrated. I had been deceived, and truth went from ignorance to denial. I felt lost. Like my friend said, I had no compass. I was like a wandering sailor, my boat was my golf and my clubs were my rudder. When I teach golf, I always ask questions to my students: What do you feel about this? Where does this go and why? What is the result of this swing?

I could ask a hundred questions. But the problem is you cannot trust your feelings, emotions, or knowledge without a solid-based foundation of truth.

But when I learned and understood the truth of His word. Then I knew who I was.

Ephesians 1:4–5: "He chose me in Him before the foundation of the world, That we would be blameless before Him in love. He predestined us to adoption as sons through Jesus Christ to Himself."

And why I am here, to be tested and to choose.

First Corinthians 10:13: "No temptation (or test) has overtaken you but such as is common to man: And God is faithful, who will not allow you to be tempted beyond what you are able, but with the temptation (test) will provide the way of escape also, so that you will be able to endure it."

The test is, I am here to choose. I believe that all people have been given free will. However, in this world mindset, our free will has been compromised by our culture and Satan's plan to rule over us. However, there is another choice. We can choose Jesus and His kingdom; we are here to choose and to learn the truth. The world does not know the truth. This world is built upon our efforts caused by shame, lies, and untruths.

The kingdom of God is built on love, grace, and truth.

John 1:14: "And the Word (Jesus) became flesh and dwelt among us, and we saw His glory, glory as of the only begotten from the Father, full of grace and truth."

John 1:12: "But as many as received Him, to them He gave the right to become children of God, even to those who believe in His name."

John 11:25–26: "Jesus said, 'I am the resurrection and the life; he who believes in Me will live even if he dies. And everyone who lives and believes in Me will never die. Do you believe?'"

Understand the Parables of God's Kingdom

All people are born with a body, soul, and spirit. The flesh will die, but the spirit will live. The question is, where will you be? Will you be sons of God in His kingdom or not? Will you receive the free gift of salvation or not? This is why we are here. Open your heart; hear and see the kingdom of God in the parables.

I love the way Jesus and the Jews teach something in two contrasting ways of seeing. They teach by using stories and parables. Some examples: In Luke 15, a man has one hundred sheep; ninety-nine are in the field, and one is lost. A woman had ten coins, and she lost one. A man had two sons; one left, and the other stayed. Two houses were built, one on sand and one on a rock.

I am including more information on parables here from the *Ryrie Study Bible*, NASB. In Mark 4:11–15: "As soon as He was alone, His followers, with the twelve, began asking Him about the parables. And He was saying to them, 'To you has been given the mystery of the kingdom of God, but those who are outside get everything in parables, so that while seeing, they may see and not perceive, and while hearing, they may hear and not understand; otherwise they might return and be forgiven.' And He said to them, 'Do you not understand this parable? How will you understand all the parables? The sower sows the word.'"

Mark 4:2: "And He was teaching them many things in parables, and was saying to them in His *teachings*."

Just as in pagan mystery religions, the initiate was instructed in the teaching of the cult, which was not revealed to outsiders, so the purpose of parables was to instruct the disciples without revealing truths to those who are outside. Parables test the spiritual responsiveness of those who hear them. A parable is a figure of speech in which a moral or spiritual truth is illustrated by an analogy drawn from everyday experiences. About one-third of our Lord's teachings were in the form of parables. Some are short sayings designed to inculcate a single truth. Others, like the sower (Mark 4:3–20), have detailed interpretations. Parables were told by Christ usually to make the truth more engaging and clearer to those who were willing to hear, but sometimes they were used to make the truth obscure to those who lacked spiritual sensitivity. Here Jesus is teaching the kingdom of God through His parables.

Mark 4:3–9: "Listen to this! Behold, the sower went out to sow; as he was sowing, some seed fell beside the road, and the birds came and ate it up. Other seed fell on the rocky ground where it did not have much soil; and immediately it sprang up because it had no depth of soil. And after the sun had risen, it was scorched; an d because it had no root, it withered away. Other seed fell among the thorns, and the thorns came up and choked it, and it yielded no crop. Other seeds fell into the good soil, and as they grew up and increased, they yielded a crop and produced thirty, sixty, and a hundredfold." And He was saying, "He who has ears to hear, let him hear."

Here Jesus took the apostles away from the crowd to explain and understand the meanings of the parables. Mark 4:15–20: "These are the ones who are beside the road where the word is sown; and when they hear, immediately Satan comes and takes away the word which has been sown to them. In a similar way, these are the ones on whom seed was sown on the rocky places, who, when they hear the word, immediately receive it with joy; and they have no firm root in themselves, but are only temporary; then, when affliction or persecution arises because of the word, immediately they fall away. And others are the ones on whom seed was sown among the thorns; these are the ones who have heard the word, but the worries of the world, and the deceitfulness of riches, and the desires for other things enter in and choke the word, and it becomes unfruitful. And those are the ones on whom seed was sown on the good soil; and they hear the word and accept it and bear fruit, thirty, sixty, and a hundredfold."

Here Jesus talks about the sower of seed = God's Word. The seed of God's Word landed in four different soils. In the first three soils, seeds landed in their minds, but the word did not become fruitful. However, the fourth seed landed in the mind and finished in their heart. This created a living fruit of God's Word.

Lamp. Mark 4:21–25: "And He was saying to them, 'A lamp is not brought to be put under a basket, is it, or under a bed? Is it not brought to be put on the lampstand? For nothing is hidden, except to be revealed, nor has anything been secret, but that it would come to light. If anyone has ears to hear, let him hear.' And He was saying to them, 'Take care what you listen to. By your standard of measure, it will be measured to you; and more will be given you besides. For whoever has, to him more shall be given; and whoever does not have, even what he has shall be taken away from him.'" One understood and was saved, and one did not understand and was lost.

Seed growing. Mark 4:26–29: "And He was saying, 'The kingdom of God is like a man who casts seed upon the soil; and he goes to bed at night and gets up by day, and the seed sprouts and grows—how, he himself does not know. The soil produces crops by itself; first the blade, then the head, then the mature grain in the head. But when the crop permits, he immediately puts in the sickle, because the harvest has come.'" The soil for the seed is to believe, which yields faith. The faith is a picture of a finished fruit: past, present, and future. You have been sanctified and set apart from this world. And God is faithful, and no one can separate us from Him.

Mustard seed. Mark 4:30–34: "And He said, 'How shall we picture the kingdom of God, or by what parable shall we present it? It is like a mustard seed, which when sown upon the soil, though it is smaller than all the seeds that are upon the soil, yet when it is sown, it grows up and becomes larger than all the garden plants and forms large branches, so that the birds of the air can rest under its shade.' With many such parables He was speaking the word to them, so far as they were able to hear it; and He did not speak to them without a parable; but He was explaining everything privately to His own disciples."

Isaiah 6:9–10: The prophecy of Isaiah is being fulfilled, which says,

You will keep on hearing—but you will not understand
You will keep on seeing—but will not perceive
For the heart of the people—Has become dull
With, their ears they scarcely—Hear
And they have closed their—Eyes
Otherwise, they would see—with their eyes
Hear with their ears
And understand with their hearts and return.

But blessed are your eyes, because they see: and your ears, because they hear.

Jesus said in John 10:26–28, "But you do not believe, because you are not of my sheep. My sheep hear My voice, and I know them, and they follow Me: and I give eternal life to them, and they will never perish; and no one will snatch them out of My hand."

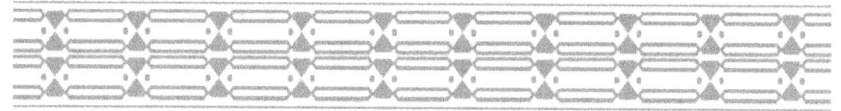

Do It

Walk in the things you have been called for.

My story:

I remember when I was still young in the church of the Open Door, they asked me to speak at a conference of churches from around the world. So I did. I told them who I was and what I have been taught: the true gospel through Grace by Faith. Therefore "if anyone is in Christ, he is a new creature; the old things passed away; behold new things have come" (2 Corinthians 5:17). I learned that the old man's, Adam's, sin is gone. And the new man, Jesus, has come. He took away my sin, and I am now in Christ, and He dwells in me, through the Holy Spirit. This is the power of the resurrection. It is finished by His blood on the cross.

My poem:

> Behold the Lord Thy God
> Creator of the light
> That we should walk by faith
> And not by worldly might
> Walk—as a brand-new creature
> Walk—with a brand-new heart
> Walk—with trust in your teacher
> And His Spirit will do His part

Progress of Sonship

In the two books of Peter, Peter states in the first book the theme of "the true grace of God" in the life of a believer. The second book has the development of faith and the denouncing of false teachers. My goal as a believer in Christ Jesus is to help people learn the truth and that the truth will set you free. Jesus says, "I am the way, the truth, and the life, and no one can see the Father except through me" (John 14:6).

Let's hear from 2 Peter 1:12: "Therefore, I will always be ready to remind you of these things, even though you already know them and have been established in the truth which is present with you."

Thank you, Lord, for the Holy Spirit. We are sons and daughters of God, Abba Father. Help us, Lord; you are always here in our presence. We know who we are; we know what we have. All truth comes from above; your Spirit dwells within us and leads us.

The last verse of 2 Peter 3:18 states, "growing in the grace and knowledge of our Lord and Savior Jesus Christ. To Him be the glory, both now and to the day of eternity. Amen."

With the power of the Holy Spirit, He leads and reminds us in His Word. If you have been saved, you are sanctified by Christ. He owns you. You have been set apart in two different places in His time. Sanctification means that, first, you are saved from this world in its shame and sin. You are given eternal life and rewards in heaven. This will be done in God's time. Second, you are saved eternally, but you will be rewarded by your works of learning and growing in grace and truth. As we have seen in 1 Corinthians 3:10–15, your works will be tested by fire. Some rewards can be lost. But salvation is not based on your works. It is a free gift from the promise of the Holy Spirit. Any works here were finished by Jesus Christ at the cross.

In this second time frame for us, we learn and grow in our faith. We are learning here with the Holy Spirit. Now I am saved. This is my time to learn and grow into who I am. I am a child of God. This is a progressive faith teaching in sonship.

Salvation

This is the fourth part of my motto: See it, know it, believe it, do it, and own it. My faith is built on Jesus Christ, and my salvation is built on His Word. This is the foundation of what I believe.

First Corinthians 3:10–11: "According to the grace of God which was given to me, like a wise master builder I laid a foundation, and another is building on it. But each man must be careful how he builds on it. For no man can lay a foundation other than the one which is laid, which is Jesus Christ." My foundation is built on four stones:

> Number 1: Jesus is the cornerstone that, with the
> Holy Spirit, leads me to the Spirit of Truth.
> Number 2 is righteousness, reckoned (paid in full)
> for me by God's grace.
> Number 3 is the knowledge of justification, and I
> have been set free from my sins. I have been
> acquitted (not guilty).
> Number 4 is sanctification, which means "to set
> apart," from the root word for saint and holy.

Now I would like to explain these words and understand why and what they are. When I became a true believer in Jesus Christ, I was just a babe, as the apostle John said, "my little children." These words were foreign to me. And as we all have to grow and learn who we really are, it will take time and patience.

So I will start with number 1: the cornerstone, the Holy Spirit, is crucial to starting a foundation of my faith. Everything has to align correctly; each stone has to be in sync with the other stones. As the parable of Jesus said, do not build a house on sand but on rock. The lead rock of your foundation of faith is from the Holy Spirit and the Spirit of Truth; it is the cornerstone of my faith.

Ephesians 1:13: "In Him, you also, after listening to the message of truth, the gospel of your salvation—having also believed, you were sealed in Him with the Holy Spirit of promise." This is a note from the *Ryrie Study Bible*, having also believed. This time of sealing coincides with the time of believing, sealed with the Holy Spirit. A seal indicates possession and security. The presence of the Holy Spirit, the seal, is the believer's guarantee of the security of their salvation. I have been sealed, and my salvation is secure.

Number 2: the stone is righteousness. How can I be so blameless in my righteousness when I was a sinner? This was one of the mysteries of God through His grace. Here is something I had to learn from the Spirit of Truth. God never lies, and His promises are always true, and I need to know this. My faith was in the promises of Jesus. My faith is in Him, not me. Now I live in Him, and He lives in me through the promise of the Holy Spirit, and we are one. So I have sinned during my life and continue to be tempted in various ways through the flesh, but because I believe and have faith, because Jesus paid the price on the cross for my sins, His righteousness is imputed to me. How can this be? It just is.

Number 3 is justification. Justification could never be based on our good works, for God requires perfect obedience, which is impossible for man. The means of justification is faith. Faith is never grounded on justification; it is the means or channel through which God's grace can impute to the believing sinner the righteousness of Christ. When we believe, all that Christ is God puts to our account; thus, we stand acquitted. Then God can justly announce the acquittal, and that pronouncement is justification.

Number 4 is about sanctification. The word *sanctify* means "to set apart." Sanctification occurs on three levels; you could say it occurs in three different levels of time. Notice and study the difference between Hebrews 8:1–13, the first covenant of the Old Testament, and Hebrews 10:1–18, the second covenant of the New Testament.

Hebrews 10:18: "Now where there is forgiveness of these things, there is no longer any offering for sin."

Matthew 5:17: "Jesus said I did not think I came to abolish the law or the Prophets, I did not come to abolish but to fulfill."

Now we are not under the law but under grace.

The first level is called positional sanctification. A believer has been set apart by his position in the family of God. Hebrews 10:10: "By this will we have been sanctified through the offering of the body of Jesus Christ once and for all."

The second level is experiential sanctification. First Peter 1:14–15: "As obedient children, do not be conformed to the former lusts which were yours in your ignorance, but like the Holy One who called you, be holy yourselves also in all your behavior." This level has to do with how we live our lives, what we do.

And the third level occurs after we die, when we see Christ, and we will become as He is. This is the ultimate or future sanctification as we are waiting for the glorification with resurrection bodies. First John 3:1–4: "What was from the beginning, what we have heard, what we have seen with our eyes, what we have looked at and touched with our hands, concerning the Word of Life—and the life was manifested, and we have seen and testify and proclaim to you the eternal life, which was with the Father and was manifested to us—what we have seen and heard we proclaim to you also, so that you too may have fellowship with us; and indeed our fellowship is with the Father and with His Son Jesus Christ. These things we write, so that your joy may be made complete."

After reading everything I've written, do you believe, as many people do, that you can lose your salvation? I firmly believe that salvation, once gained, cannot be lost. For in order to lose one's salvation, all of these works of God would have to be undone, and the Bible nowhere even hints that this is possible. Salvation is conditioned solely on faith in Jesus Christ. *Faith*, or *belief*, is stated nearly two hundred times as the single condition in the New Testament. Faith must be placed in Christ, who paid for our sins on the cross, who suffered the punishment that we deserved, and who set us free. It is not easy to believe someone you don't know and have never seen about the most important matter of eternal destiny, but this is the only way to be saved.

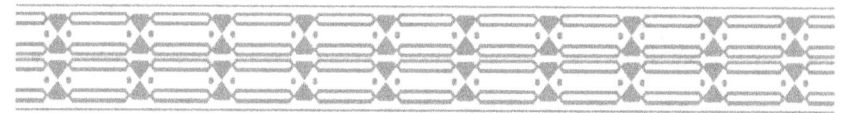

Own It

My will and testament
Most importantly,
I remember God. I remember with every passing day,
the gifts that He has given me.
You have given me a new heart;
You have given me life and more time.
Thank You, Lord, for time.
Whatever Your will is,
whatever my time is, let me use it with You.
My will and Your will are one.

My poem:

You told me not to fear
To get strength from you on High
Before—I listened with my ear
But now—I see you with my eye
Trust not in things both seen and heard
I am a God who cannot lie
Through the Gospel power in my Word
I will meet you in the sky

My Heart

After I received a new transplanted heart in 2012 and things started to slow down, I knew I had to get more active. Rehab was first; I really had no choice. But then after a few months, there was a gnawing in my spirit. I was given a new heart but also more time. I felt I had to do something, to start the project of sharing God's faithfulness in my life. After about four months of rehab, I was ready. I went back to one of my favorite scriptures: Repent = change your mind.

Romans 12:2: "And do not be conformed to this world, but be transformed by the renewing of your mind, so that you may prove what the will of God is, that which is good and acceptable and perfect."

When I pray and study His Word, He (the Holy Spirit) usually leads me to a scripture. However, it never stops there, because I always test myself in what I am hearing. Is it from inside or from outside of me? Therefore, I need to go deeper. Okay, it is from inside. But then what spirit—Holy Spirit or my spirit? I have been here before, and I have always struggled here. I always ask God, "Yes or no?" But most of the time I get, "Maybe."

In 1982, when I went back for God, I asked, "Are you real?" Maybe.

In 1995, my wife wanted a divorce. Should I agree? Maybe.

In 1996, I had a dream, a poem. What is this? Should I do something? Maybe.

So then I always end up in 1 Corinthians 12:4, 11: "Now there are varieties of gifts, but the same Spirit... And to another the effecting of miracles, and to another prophecy, and to another distinguishing of spirits, to another various kinds of tongues, and to another the interpretation of tongues." Okay. Do I understand this? Maybe.

In 2012: Lord, should I receive another heart or let it go to another person? Maybe. But this time I understood: Let go and let God. Jesus said, when He knew He was going to die, "My Father, if it is possible, let this cup pass from Me; yet not as I will, but as You will" (Luke 22:42).

More = less and less = more. How can this be? This is upside-down thinking. The Holy Spirit says, "Let go of this world and spend more time with God. Let go and let God."

First Corinthians 2:12–14: "Now we have received, not the spirit of the world, but the Spirit who is from God, so that we may know the things freely given to us by God, which things we also speak, not in words taught by human wisdom, but in those taught by the Spirit, combining spiritual thoughts with spiritual words. But a natural man does not accept the things of the Spirit of God, for they are foolishness to him; and he cannot understand them because they are spiritually appraised."

Therefore, this is why I have written this story. Open your eyes and see the truth, and open your ears to hear and learn the wisdom of the Holy Spirit. And say yes, I will choose Jesus, my Savior and Lord.

Matthew 22:37–39: "You shall love the Lord your God with all your heart, and with all your soul, and with all your mind." This is the great and foremost commandment. The second is: "You shall love your neighbor as yourself."

Jesus said in John 14:23–24, "If anyone loves Me, he will keep My word; and My Father will love him, and We will come to him and make Our abode with him." Here Jesus talks about His Father's love as conditioned on our knowledge and obedience to His Word. "He who does not love Me does not keep My words; and the word which you hear is not Mine, but the Father's who sent Me." This is something that breaks my heart for many Christians. They will say, "Yes, I love Jesus," but the Bible was written for a past time, and we have moved now into a new way of thinking. Now, with the science and tech knowledge of today, we have to become more secular and social and don't believe God's Word. The wise became fools, but the fools became wise.

John 14:15–17: "If you love Me, you will keep My commandments. I will ask the Father, and He will give you another Helper that He may be with you forever; that is, the Spirit of truth, whom the world cannot receive because it does not see Him or know Him. But you know Him because He abides with you and will be in you."

John 14:25–26: "These things I have spoken to you while abiding with you." Then, after the power of the resurrection of Christ: "But the Helper, the Holy Spirit, whom the Father will send in My name, He will teach you all things and bring to your remembrance all that I said to you."

Therefore, if you believe in your heart, your soul, and your mind; if Jesus is the Son of Man and the Son of God; if you believe His Word is true, then you will abide in Him as He is in His Father.

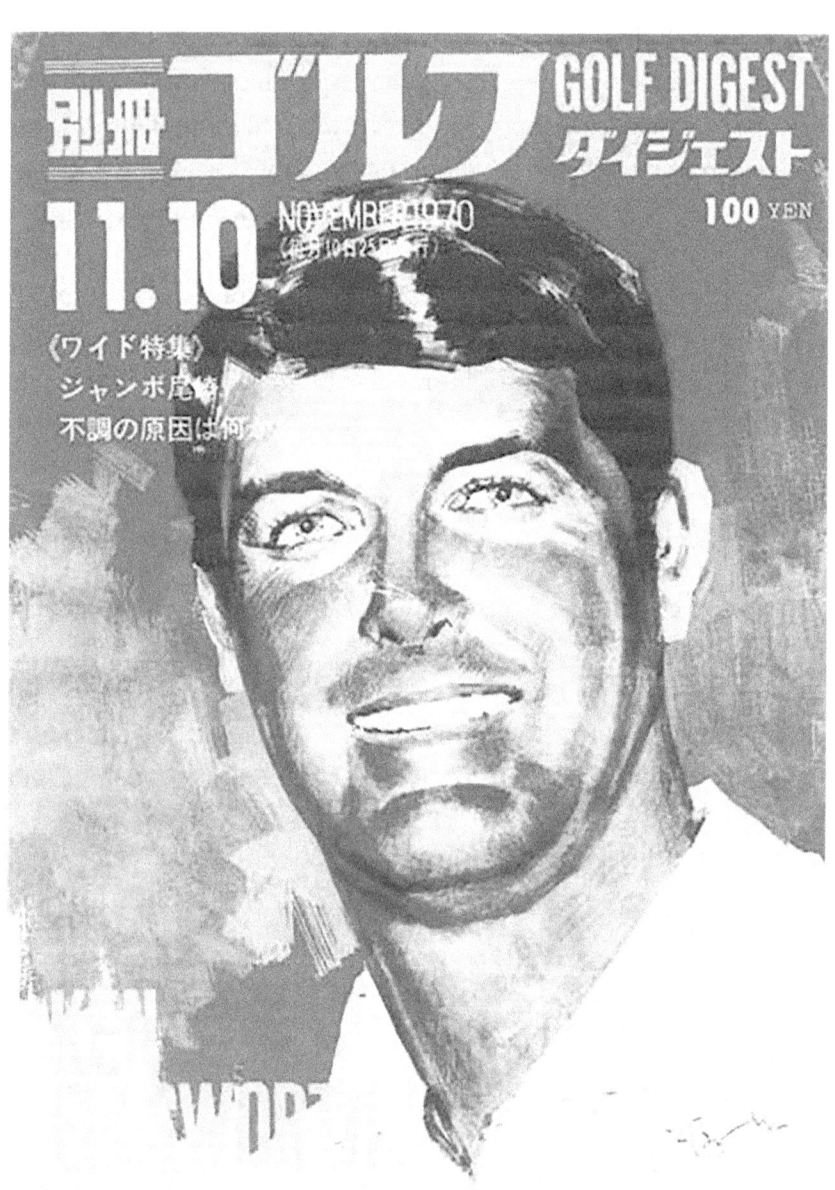

別冊 ゴルフ GOLF DIGEST
ダイジェスト

11.10

NOVEMBER 1970
(毎月10と25日発行)

100 YEN

〈ワイド特集〉
ジャンボ尾崎
不調の原因は何か

日本で初めて味わう"優勝"

■ケン・エルスワース（米国）謝永を制す

B・S・ゴルフ・トーナメント
45年11月4・5日
ブリデストンCC
（6630ヤード・パー72）
72ホール・ストローク・プレー

最終ホール　見事なバンカー・ショット

最終ラウンド、16番でK・エ
ルスワースと御永忠谷が6に10
アンダーで並んだ。

勝負は残り2ホールにかけら
れ17番、ショート・ホールへ。
御に手痛い3パットのボギー
が待っていた。

エルスワースは手堅くパー。
気落ちしたのか、御に悪い
いえるが18番でも大崩しい
ご丁寧で御の気落ちに乗じたエ
ルスワースが優勝を飾り、賞金
100万円と初日のコース・レ
コード賞10万円を獲得した。

栄光学生のベスト5には入っ
たが、御藤は認めてだという・
御後藤を飾った「日本の歌」
は一生エルスワースの記憶に残
るだろう。（記録は280頁）

88

は自成して2位に得まる

見せた
ガッツ
トーナメント

ン・エルスワース、東海の万名my(?)監と接怒って総裁第を握る

東海クラシックで157を叩き
二日目にしてあえなく失格したケ
ン・エルスワース。"本場ツアー・
プロの惨威夫呼の集本人として信
玉にあがったが、東海終了の三日
後に鮮やかによみがえった。
競技は今年から規模が……
大き、……

傷のないケンにとって、
ホールはまさに苦戦、

た、

必死の広？

ン、潮七。

り、

ブリヂストン トーナメント

本場アメリカから来日中のケン・エルスワース、グリア・ジョーンズの新鋭2人を加えてのブリヂストントーナメントは、この二人に謙永都橋岡周がからみ、涼しい試合展開を見せた。

初日、65のコース・レコードをマークしたエルスワースに対し謙が最終ラウンドに入り謙が猛進、一時は逆転して逃げ切りを思わせた。ところが本場アメリカでも期待を集めているエルスワースは、謙のベースにまきこまれずバーディで反撃。

タイのまま進んだ17番で謙が3パットで自滅。結局エルスワースが2ストローク差で謙を押え、優勝賞金100万円を獲得した。三位は橋岡とジョーンズが4ストローク差で分け合った。
（11/4~5、ブリヂストンCC）

橋岡（右）、謙（中央）のベテランと組んだエルスワースだったが自己のペースを守り抜いた。

My Golf History

Division 1 All-American.
1st Place finishes in several college events.
Competed on PGA Tour for 7 years.
5th Place - Hawaiian Open 1968.
7th Place - Los Angeles Open 1969.
1st Place - Bridgestone Classic in Japan 1970.

Other Professional events not on the PGA Tour:

1st Place - Nevada 1977.
1st Place - Utah 1978.
1st Place - PGA Wisconsin Match Play Champions 1981.

Head Professional at Ville du Farc G.C. WI 1979-1980.
Head Professional at Edina C.C. MN 1981-1989.
Director of Instruction for Natural Golf 1995-2000.
Featured 4 times on the "Academy Live with Natural Golf" on the Golf Channel.
Inducted into Natural Golf Hall of Fame.
Named "Top One Hundred Golf Teachers".
Contributed to Publication of "Lifetime of Better Golf".
As a Natural Golf player, I played in two Senior Tour events including the PGA Senior Championship.
A "Life member of the PGA" for 48 years.

About the Author

Why did I write this?

It was July 17, 2012; my heart was failing. The doctors said that I needed a heart—a transplanted heart from a donor. How could this be? How could this be? Why me? I was sixty-nine years old; I had run a good race, and I was at peace with myself and my Creator. Should I receive a heart, or should I let it go to another person? I have done my best. What should I do?

There are two parts to this story. I assume that you will read the first part of this book and my testament of what I did. My story is all about how I became a follower of Jesus Christ. The second part is what I have learned and how and why I learned it.

Born June 22, 1943, I was baptized in a Lutheran church; I went to church religiously and was thrilled to do the right things. But after high school and college, I just wandered off. Like the story in Matthew 15:11, the prodigal son, I knew about Jesus, but I did not know him. For me, everything was about sports—first basketball, then golf. Golf was my source, and Jesus was a resource. This is why I drafted this book. Jesus said in John 8:32, "And you will know the truth, and the truth will make you free."

God became my source, and golf became my resource.